P9-DDU-304

DIANA, PRINCESS OF WALES

YOUNG ROYALTY

By Beatrice Gormley

Aladdin Paperbacks
New York London Toronto Sydney

To the Gormley princesses:
Kit, Margaret, and Mary Rose

ALADDIN PAPERBACKS
An imprint of Simon & Schuster Children's Publishing Division
1230 Avenue of the Americas, New York, NY 10020
Text copyright © 2005 by Beatrice Gormley
All rights reserved, including the right of reproduction in whole or in
part in any form.
CHILDHOOD OF WORLD FIGURES is a registered trademark
of Simon & Schuster, Inc.
ALADDIN PAPERBACKS and colophon are trademarks
of Simon & Schuster, Inc.
Designed by Lisa Vega
The text of this book was set in Aldine721 BT.
Manufactured in the United States of America
First Aladdin Paperbacks edition August 2005
10 9 8 7 6 5 4 3
Library of Congress Control Number 2004113724
ISBN-13: 978-1-4169-0021-4
ISBN-10: 1-4169-0021-7

CONTENTS

CHAPTER 1
TEA WITH THE PRINCES

"Not hair-wash time again!" protested the little girl.

"Now Diana, think how pretty you'll be with lovely, clean—" the girl's nanny said, trying to guide her into the bathroom. But Diana slipped from her grasp and ran down the hall.

"I'll not chase you all over the house," warned Nanny Thompson as she followed. That made Diana giggle, because Nanny *was* chasing her. She headed for the top of the stairs and the white wrought-iron banister. Diana vaulted onto the banister and slid down, still giggling. Let Nanny try this!

It was midwinter in Norfolk, England, a few days after Christmas 1966. Diana Spencer, five years old, and her two-year-old brother, Charlie,

1

had been invited to tea with their neighbors' children. The Spencers lived in Park House, at the edge of an estate called Sandringham. Their neighbors, the owners of the estate, were the Windsors. They were also known as Queen Elizabeth II of England and her husband, Prince Philip, the Duke of Edinburgh. Diana and Charles's hosts for tea would be the Windsors' younger boys, Prince Andrew and Prince Edward.

At the bottom of the stone stairs Diana turned to see her sister Sarah coming in the door. Sarah, the oldest of the Spencer children at eleven, had just finished riding. She had her jodhpurs and boots on, and her face was pink. Strands of red hair escaped from under her riding hat.

"Diana, you'd better go have your bath," said Sarah. "You can't be late for royalty—don't you know that?" In a teasing tone she added, "Besides, if you keep Prince Andrew waiting, he won't want to marry you when you grow up."

Diana knew the part about marrying was a joke, but she let Nanny catch her and shepherd her back up to the nursery rooms. Diana did like it after hair-wash, when her long blond hair was combed and silky clean. Nanny buttoned the back of Diana's new blue velvet dress and buckled her party shoes. Then they set off for the "big house," as Diana called the Windsors'.

Diana could have walked to Sandringham House, with Nanny pushing Charlie in the pram, if they hadn't been all dressed up. But on this chilly December afternoon they climbed into the car with Nanny, and the Spencers' chauffeur drove them to the royal mansion. It was an enormous brick building, ten times as big as Park House.

A footman met Nanny and the two Spencer children at the front entrance and showed them upstairs to the nursery floor. There, Mabel Anderson, the royal nanny, took over.

The princes were dressed up, too, wearing ties and jackets with their short pants. "Good afternoon, Your Royal Highnesses," said Diana. She curtsied without even being reminded by Nanny.

"Good afternoon, Miss Spencer," said Prince Andrew, six years old. Prince Edward and Diana's brother, both two years old, were too little to have proper manners.

The children ate their meal sitting at a table, while another footman served. As they drank their milk and ate their buttered toast with honey, Diana and Andrew began to laugh at their little brothers.

Prince Edward seemed to like the honey very much. He pressed a piece of toast to his face, to lick the honey off. Then he wiped his sticky hands on his fair hair. Diana and Andrew exchanged glances and giggled.

An older boy, almost grown up, appeared at the nursery door. He gave Nanny Anderson a kiss on the cheek. "A tea party!" he exclaimed. "Why wasn't I invited?"

"Charles," Andrew greeted him, "look at Edward!"

"What's this?" asked Prince Charles, making a face of mock horror at his youngest brother. "Old Edward Bear has got into the honey pot again, eh?" He turned to Diana. "Good afternoon, Miss Spencer. I hope you're having a nice tea."

"Yes, thank you, Your Royal Highness," answered Diana through her giggles. She slipped down from her chair for a moment to curtsy. The older prince had a mild, pleasant look. His ears were large and stuck out a bit under his curly dark brown hair. With a wave good-bye, he was gone again.

After the meal, the princes' nanny cleaned up the two littlest boys. Andrew said to Diana, "Let's play hide-and-seek."

Diana agreed, except she wanted to be the one to hide and so did Andrew. Luckily Andrew's mother appeared just then to look in on the children's tea.

"Good afternoon, Your Majesty," said Diana, curtsying again. The queen was a pretty woman, with pink cheeks and twinkly blue eyes. *Not as*

5

pretty as my mother, though, Diana thought. Frances Spencer was tall, slim, and blond.

At Andrew's begging, the queen agreed to be "it."

"Hooray!" shouted Andrew. "Close your eyes and count to thirty, Mummy."

The queen put her hands over her eyes and started counting, "Five, ten—"

"Not by fives!" protested Andrew. Holding Diana's hand, he pulled her into the hall.

After hide-and-seek, Nanny Thompson came up from the servants' common room to fetch the Spencer children. On the drive back to Park House she asked Diana, "Did you have a nice tea with Prince Andrew and Prince Edward, dear?"

"Tea was quite nice," answered Diana. She paused, trying to think why it had been harder than usual to have fun. Maybe it was Sandringham House itself. "But I don't like that big, ugly house."

With a gasp, Nanny turned from the front seat to stare. "What a way to talk! Any other little girl in the world would jump at the chance to have tea with the princes."

Nanny didn't understand, and Diana couldn't really explain what she meant. But she knew what she had felt: a heavy dullness that hung in the air where the princes lived.

A few months later, on a rainy morning at Park House, Diana followed the sound of piano notes into the music room. She knew it would be Grandmother Ruth at the grand piano. Sarah took piano lessons, and her teacher said she was quite good. But the rich, full sound that Grandmother's fingers drew from the piano was something else entirely.

Grandmother Ruth, Mummy's mother, had come to Park House for a visit. She was also called Lady Fermoy because her husband had been Baron Fermoy. She was lady-in-waiting to the Queen Mother, Prince Andrew and Edward's grandmother. That meant she spent most of her time with the royal court, keeping the Queen Mother company.

Diana looked out the windows of the music room at the wet tennis court. Then she began to stroll around the room, gazing at the photographs. That was Daddy in uniform with his regiment, the Scots Guards. That was Daddy and Mummy with little Sarah and baby Jane, before Diana was born. And this one, of a man and woman arm-in-arm in front of a church, was Mummy and Daddy getting married.

As Diana studied the black-and-white picture, Grandmother Ruth played a final trill and chord. "Good morning, Diana." She came over to look at the photo with her. "Now *that* was a day to remember."

"Mummy's so beautiful," said Diana. The young woman in the photo wore a long white dress, and a white veil floated behind her tiara-crowned head.

"Yes, Frances made quite a stir in society the year she came out, in nineteen fifty-four. The papers called her wedding to Johnny, your daddy, *the* wedding of the year," said her grandmother with satisfaction. "Your father was not only Viscount Althorp—the next Earl Spencer—but also equerry to the queen, a court attendant, at the time." She pointed to the church in the picture. "They were married in Westminster Abbey, in London."

"Did the queen come to the wedding?" asked Diana.

"Oh yes, and Prince Philip, and of course my dear friend the Queen Mother." Grandmother Ruth smiled. "There were more than one thousand guests. The reception was held at St. James's Palace."

Diana looked from the picture to her grandmother. Grandmother Ruth wasn't soft and kind like Daddy's mother, Grandmother Cynthia, but she was interesting. She pronounced the words "equerry to the Queen," "Westminster Abbey," and "St. James's Palace" as if they tasted delicious in her mouth.

Then Diana remembered something her sister Sarah had said. "If I married Prince Andrew, would our wedding be in Westminster Abbey?"

Grandmother Ruth didn't laugh at the idea of Diana marrying the prince. In fact, she looked pleased. "Very likely. And then you'd be the Duchess of York, wouldn't you?"

By the next summer, Nanny Janet Thompson had left the Spencers. Diana overheard Nanny telling her mother why. Sarah had refused to tidy her room, and then she had said something rude to Nanny. It was the last straw, Nanny said.

That was upsetting enough. But one afternoon, before the new nanny arrived, Diana overheard something much worse. It was her parents' angry voices in the drawing room. Diana peeked in the open door. They were turned away from her, and she slipped behind a drapery.

Diana didn't really understand what they were quarreling about. Her mother said something scornful about the Sandringham Cattle Show. Her father said something about London in a quiet, mean voice. Her mother answered him in a light, cold voice. Their voices went on, back and forth, as if they were throwing gravel at each other. Diana thought somebody ought to say, "Stop this at once!" But there was no one to say that to her mummy and daddy.

Finally, Frances Spencer's heels clicked across the floor, and Diana glimpsed her walking out the door. Diana's father sighed heavily and walked around the room. Then he left too.

Diana ran down to the kitchen, brushing past Jane on the stairs. "What's gotten into you?" asked Jane, but Diana didn't answer.

In the kitchen, Diana threw herself at the cook. The woman was stirring something on the stove, but she put her free arm around Diana. "What is it, dear? I'm sure it's nothing to cry about."

Diana knew there *was* something to cry about, but she didn't want to talk about it. The cook sat her at the kitchen table and gave her a cup of cocoa and some chocolate biscuits, and after a while Diana felt a little better.

A few days later another nanny took Janet Thompson's place, but she didn't stay long. "Why ever is this nanny leaving?" murmured Sarah to Jane. "I didn't say boo to her. Was it because our Charlie is such a little pig? Or was it because Diana threw Nanny's clothes out on the roof?"

"Diana's gotten as naughty as you," agreed Jane with a laugh.

Diana climbed into a tree near the front drive and watched the chauffeur put the nanny's suitcase into the car. This nanny had deserved to have tricks played on her. She'd kept a wooden spoon in her pocket to hit Diana and Charlie on the head if they misbehaved.

Still, now that the woman was leaving, Diana felt rather sorry that the nanny didn't like her. As the car started off toward the train station, Diana called, "Good-bye!" and gave a friendly wave. But the nanny didn't wave back.

In September there were more changes in the Spencer household. Sarah and Jane went off to boarding school at West Heath. And Frances Spencer went off to London. "Mummy's going to try living in the city for a while," she said brightly to Diana and Charlie. "Just the three of us and Nanny." The day after she left, Diana and her brother, accompanied by their nanny, took the train to London.

Johnny Spencer came to the train station to see Diana and Charlie off. "I need to stay and look after the cattle, but I'll come to visit you on the weekends," he promised. "We'll go to the zoo and see the elephant—won't that be jolly?"

Frances Spencer now had an apartment on Cadogan Place, in Belgravia, a nice section of London. Diana went to a day school, and Charlie to a kindergarten. On weekends their father picked them up. Johnny and Frances were polite to each other, but Diana noticed that her mother often had tears in her eyes. And there were new lines around her father's mouth.

December came, and the school term

ended. Diana, Charlie, and their mother rode the train to Norfolk to spend Christmas at Park House. Diana was glad—she was sure her mother would decide to stay, once she got back to Park House. London was interesting in a way, but Diana had missed Norfolk. At Park House, she could run outside without waiting for a grown-up to take her. She could climb trees, run over the fields with the dogs, and visit the stables and feed carrots to the horses. Sarah and Jane were home from school too—everything was the way it should be.

On Christmas Day the children got piles of presents, as usual. Diana had asked for another stuffed animal, and sure enough Father Christmas had brought her a lovely fuzzy green hippo. Right after breakfast she put the hippo into her doll pram, wrapped up against the cold, and wheeled him around the drive. She ate all the chocolates she wanted to.

But only a few days later, everything turned dreadful. On that gray morning, Diana walked slowly down the front stairs. Today, she didn't feel like sliding. She sat down on the bottom step, clutching the railings, and leaned her head against them. Footsteps passed her going up the stairs and coming down again, but she didn't turn her head. Out of the corner of her eye she saw the servants' feet and the bags and suitcases they carried. Mummy's suitcases.

Finally, Diana heard her mother's step. She smelled her mother's scent, verbena cologne, as Frances Spencer sat down beside her. "Diana, I'm going back to London now."

Diana knew perfectly well what her mother meant, but she said, "All right, Mummy. I'll go pack my animals."

"No, dear." Her mother's voice was choked. "I have to go by myself. Daddy says you and Charlie are to stay here."

"Don't go," said Diana in a small voice.

Her mother gave her a squeeze, but she said, "Darling, I have to go. It's better for Daddy and Mummy not to live together. You see, we can't be happy together."

With a final kiss, Frances Spencer got up

and hurried out the front door. Diana stayed on the bottom step, feeling the cold stone and the cold iron railings. She heard footsteps crunching the gravel drive, and a car door slammed. The car engine started, and wheels rolled over the gravel.

Then there was silence. The silence seemed to go on and on, as if Diana were the only person in the whole cold world. She sat there for a long time.

Diana finally got up and climbed the stairs to her nursery room. She looked at the stuffed animals on her bed. They seemed cold, too, in spite of their fur. Going to Charlie's room, she found his baby clothes in the bottom drawer of his dresser. She brought a stack of the little shirts and sweaters and trousers back to her room. Murmuring softly to her animals, she began to dress the teddy bear. "All nice and warm!" she said, kissing his nose.

CHAPTER 2
TO MUMMY AND DADDY

After the Christmas holidays, Diana and her brother Charlie started at a school in King's Lynn, the nearby village. Diana liked Miss Lowe, the headmistress of Silfield School, and Miss Lowe seemed to like the way Diana helped with the littlest children.

Diana's favorite class was art class, especially painting. One day she stood at her easel, wearing an old shirt of her father's for a painting smock over her red and gray school uniform. She was putting the finishing touches on a picture of her black-and-white dog Jill running across a green field. Diana was pleased with the way the dog's ears had turned out.

Hearing someone come up behind her, Diana turned to see a girl named Sylvia. Sylvia wasn't especially nice to Diana. But now, Diana thought, Sylvia must be admiring her picture. "That's my dog Jill," she explained. "She's an English springer spaniel. See her ears flopping up and down?"

Sylvia put her hands on her hips. "You can't sign your picture 'To Mummy and Daddy,'" she said.

Diana was taken aback. Her face got warm. "Yes, I can."

"No, you can't." The other girl looked smug. "*Your* mum and dad don't live together, so they can't share."

Diana felt as if Sylvia had slapped her. She burst into tears. Sylvia looked alarmed, as if she hadn't meant to be quite *that* mean, and she scuttled back to her own easel.

The art teacher rushed to Diana and put an arm around her. "What's the matter, dear? You can't be crying about your picture—it's a lovely picture of your dog."

Diana finally wiped her tears and blew her nose, but she wouldn't say why she was crying.

18

It was too awful to talk about. She thought she must be the only girl in Silfield School whose parents didn't live together.

Otherwise Diana liked Silfield. Miss Lowe praised Diana for her reading and handwriting, and for her nice manners. When Diana stood up in class to read aloud for Miss Lowe, she leaned against her—a happy feeling.

With Sarah and Jane off at boarding school, Diana was the oldest at home. She missed her sisters, but on the other hand, it was her turn to be top dog. Now she'd be the one to choose the TV programs she liked best, like *The Magic Roundabout*.

Also, Diana felt it was her turn to be the best. Naturally Sarah and Jane, six and four years older than Diana, could ride and swim and play the piano better than she could. But Charlie was three years younger, so Diana expected to be better at everything than *he* was. She was bigger and stronger, and she was certainly braver. Why, Charlie was even frightened by the new Disney movie *Chitty Chitty*

19

Bang Bang, which they'd seen at the San-dringham House private theater.

However, Charlie was turning out to be very clever. Diana had heard Charlie's teacher telling her father about his marvelous progress at Silfield. And a few days earlier, when Diana took her brother to the sweet shop in King's Lynn, Charlie had counted out exactly the right coins to give the clerk. "Aren't you a clever little chap!" said the sweet shop woman.

Diana felt a pang. She'd never even thought of figuring out the right change. It was so easy to smile, hand the clerk her money, and take whatever change she was given. No one had ever said to Diana, "Aren't you a clever little girl!"

Worse, Charlie was starting to hold his clever-ness over his sister. One day he caught sight of her arithmetic homework paper, dotted with red X's on the wrong answers. That afternoon when Daddy picked them up from school, Charlie announced, "Diana's slow. Diana's like Brian the stupid snail on *The Magic Roundabout*!"

"You mustn't talk that way about your sister," said their father sternly.

As soon as they got home, Diana went down to the kitchen and made a cup of tea to take to her father. "Here you are, Daddy," she said as she carried the cup into his study. "Just the way you like it, with milk and one sugar." Charlie might be a clever little chap, but *she* was the one who could take care of Daddy.

The next weekend, when Diana and Charlie went to London to visit their mother, Charlie did it again. The nanny was in the kitchen, fixing their supper. Frances and the children curled up on the sofa in the drawing room to watch TV. It was time for *The Magic Roundabout,* which their mother liked even though it was a children's program.

As the beginning merry-go-round music played on the TV, Diana chattered away to her mother about the train ride from Norfolk to London. Suddenly Charlie chanted in her ear in a low voice, "Brian, Brian, Brian."

"Shut up!" Diana pinched Charlie, making him squeal.

Of course their mother wanted to know why they were squabbling. Charlie tried to pretend that he'd said "Diane," not "Brian," but he couldn't hide a smile. "Charlie," said Frances, "I will not have my children calling each other names."

As soon as their mother went into the kitchen, Diana hissed at Charlie, "See if I ever share my sweets with you again! Or match your socks for you, or help you climb the big tree."

When the weekend was over, Diana and her brother returned to Norfolk and Park House. That night Diana woke up with her heart beating hard, frightened before she even knew what was happening.

It was a storm. Lightning flickered outside her windows, and thunder crashed. Again, lightning flared, showing Diana's stuffed animals wide-eyed on either side of her. On the night table her guinea pig huddled in the shavings on the floor of his cage.

Diana was leaning over to comfort the guinea pig when she heard someone sobbing down the hall. "Mummy, Mummy!" That was Charlie. Nanny was supposed to look after him at night, but it was her day off.

Slipping out of bed, Diana ran to Charlie's room. In the light from the hall, her brother was only a lump under the covers. But when she climbed onto his bed, he popped out and clutched at her.

"There, there," said Diana in the soothing tone her mother used. She put her arms around him, and he buried his head in her shoulder. "It's all right. It's all right."

Diana stroked Charlie's hair and rubbed his back. In this moment there seemed to be a warm glow around just the two of them, and she felt calm and safe. She waited there on her brother's bed until he quieted and fell back asleep. Pulling the covers up to his chin, she went back to her own bed. She picked up her guinea pig from his cage and petted him until he stopped trembling. Then she climbed into bed carefully, so as not to disturb her stuffed animals.

On Diana's seventh birthday, July 1, 1968, her father arranged to have a camel brought to Park House from the nearby Dudley Zoo. The camel, named Bert, was a shambling, bumpy animal. He gazed down his nose at Diana and her friends, making them laugh. Bert's keeper had him kneel and give each child a camel ride—in honor of Diana.

"This is a special treat for you," Johnny Spencer told Diana, "because you've been trying so hard at school." As Diana perched up on Bert, giggles bubbling out of her throat, her father snapped picture after picture.

At the end of the afternoon, the camel and all the guests left. "Thank you for a lovely birthday, Daddy," said Diana. But she felt somehow empty, in spite of all the cake she'd eaten. Going into the music room, she stared at the picture of her mother and father on their wedding day. They'd looked so happy, then.

* ★ * ★

For Easter 1969, Johnny Spencer took all four of his children to Althorp, the estate in Northamptonshire where the Spencers had lived for hundreds of years. They rode the train to Northampton, the town nearest Althorp. There a chauffeur picked them up in Earl Spencer's glossy dark green Rolls-Royce.

As the car pulled up in front of the huge, forbidding gray country house, Diana glanced at her father. He looked like a schoolboy being sent to the headmaster for punishment. But then Grandmother Cynthia appeared at the front doors, and his face brightened for a moment.

Grandmother Cynthia's silver hair, waving around her face, set off her clear blue eyes. She hugged each of them as if she didn't know whom to hug first. But as Diana clung to her, she gave her an extra hug. "Well, Diana! You certainly have grown into a lovely big girl."

Then the five of them entered the house, to be greeted by Grandfather Spencer. The old man stood in the middle of the entrance hall, unsmiling. He shook each one's hand in turn, from his son down to Charlie.

Diana knew she was supposed to look her grandfather in the eye, but her glance fluttered down to the black-and-white marble floor. She was relieved to go off to the children's rooms with the nanny. Passing the portrait gallery off the main staircase, she caught sight of a painting of Grandfather Spencer. He was much younger in the portrait, and his hair and mustache were reddish brown instead of gray. But he had exactly the same way of looking down his nose.

On Easter morning they all went to the church in the village, Great Brington. Earl Spencer had his own pew at the front of the church. After the service Diana's grandfather pointed out the stone effigies along the inside of the church. "These are your ancestors, children. That one is Robert, the first Lord Spencer."

Diana followed her grandfather's pointing

forefinger to the images of the long-ago Spencers. When you died, she thought, you turned to stone—if you were very important.

After church, the children hunted for the colored eggs that Grandmother Cynthia had hidden in the gardens. Grandfather Spencer went off to his library, but Diana's father ran around the shrubs and beds of daffodils with his mother and the children. The glum look that had come over him when he arrived at Althorp dissolved in laughing. Diana helped Charlie fill his basket.

The next morning Grandmother Cynthia went to visit a poor woman in the village. "Would you come with me, Diana?" she asked as she set a hat on her silver hair. "I know it would make her glad to see you."

At the cottage, Grandmother Cynthia let Diana carry in a bunch of sweet peas from her cutting garden at Althorp. She herself brought a basket of Althorp delicacies: homemade marmalade, a crock of sweet butter.

Diana watched Grandmother Cynthia sit

down by the woman's wheelchair and take her hand. Her grandmother was Countess Spencer, but she never seemed to be thinking about her title. As she spoke in a warm, quiet voice, the other woman's face lit up.

Moving close to the wheelchair, Diana held out the bouquet with a smile. The woman sniffed the sweet peas and beamed at Diana. "Aren't you an English rose, just like your granny!"

Diana's grandmother smiled lovingly at her, and Diana was proud. It was a fine thing to be a Spencer and turn to stone when you died, she supposed. But she would much rather be a rose and make people happy.

CHAPTER 3
THE ARISTOCATS

Diana's eighth birthday was special, although not in the same way as the seventh. On July 1, 1969, Prince Charles was being invested—or installed with a grand ceremony—as the Prince of Wales. Prince Charles was the eldest son of the Queen of England, and he was almost twenty-one.

All the children and teachers at Silfield School gathered around the television to watch the ceremony at Caernarvon Castle in Wales. "Just think, boys and girls," said Miss Lowe, "two hundred million people around the world are watching with us."

On the small black-and-white screen, Prince Charles stepped out of a tower, wearing his ceremonial uniform. He knelt on a cushion before Queen Elizabeth, the same lady who sometimes waved at Diana as she rode her horse past Park House. The queen placed a coronet on Prince Charles's head, a gold ring on his finger, and an ermine mantel on his shoulders. She spoke words that sounded almost like a marriage ceremony: "Our most dear Son Charles Philip Arthur George . . . We do ennoble and invest with the said Principality and Earldom . . ."

Leading her son to the balcony, the queen presented Charles to the waiting crowds. Trumpets blared, and a great cheer rose up to greet the new Prince of Wales.

At Silfield School, Diana's mind wandered to her mother, who also had a new title now. When she was married to Johnny Spencer, Viscount Althorp, she had been Lady Althorp. She had married her new husband, Peter Shand Kydd, last month, and now she was just Mrs. Shand Kydd. Grandmother Ruth was very angry with Mummy about this, and Sarah said they weren't speaking to each other any longer.

The last time Diana visited her mother in London, she had met Peter Shand Kydd. He seemed very nice—but how strange to see her mother with another man! "I am so happy now, darling," Frances told Diana privately. "You see, Peter and I really, really love each other."

Now, glancing across the schoolroom at the headmistress, Diana saw tears shining in Miss Lowe's eyes. Her own eyes smarted—but she wasn't sure why.

That autumn, Sarah and Jane came home from boarding school for half-term holiday. This was Diana's chance to wait on Sarah. She brought her older sister a cup of tea in the morning, ironed her jeans, and polished her riding boots. "I didn't realize you were training to be a lady's maid, Diana," Sarah teased her. But Diana thought she seemed pleased.

One morning, when the sky was a clear pale

blue over the Sandringham parkland, the three girls went out riding. "Diana can't keep up with us," protested Jane. But Sarah said, "Oh, let her come."

The groom held Diana's pony, Romilly, as she climbed the mounting block. "Don't let him forget who's the boss, miss," he reminded Diana.

Diana blushed and gathered the reins. The last time Diana went riding, the groom had gone out with her. With the groom riding ahead, Diana's pony had trotted for a few strides and then slowed to a walk. The walk turned into an amble as he turned from side to side to snatch mouthfuls of grass. As Diana commanded and pleaded, Romilly twitched his ears. But clearly he didn't think he had to obey her.

Finally the pony had lifted his head, seeming to notice that his friend the groom's horse was out of sight. With a burst of speed, he trotted off down the bridle path. Diana tried everything she'd been taught about guiding her mount, but finally she'd given up and let him follow the groom's horse.

Diana knew this was the wrong way to ride, but she wished she could just be friends with her pony. She was good at making friends with animals as well as with people. Even grumpy Marmalade, the Spencers' orange cat, who scratched and nipped everyone else, let Diana pet him.

Today, riding with her sisters, Diana was determined to be different. She pretended she was Sarah. Sarah's horse would never forget who was the boss. Nudging Romilly from a walk into a trot, she followed her sisters through a stand of silver birch trees.

I've got it! thought Diana. Yes, this was the feeling. It was like swimming, where the water was her friend; it held her up, and she moved with it. "I love you, Romilly," she told the pony. Romilly loved her, too; she could feel it.

Ahead, Sarah remarked to Jane, "We might see the queen out riding today. The royal family's in residence." Coming to a hawthorn hedge,

Sarah and her horse floated over it. Jane followed, not quite as gracefully.

Diana's pony moved smoothly into a canter, and Diana was sure they were going to sail over the hedge, too. "Look at me!" she called to her sisters.

Suddenly Diana was sailing, but not on the pony. There was a long moment when she seemed to hang in the air with time to notice everything, even a little spiderweb in the top of the hedge. Ahead, her sisters turned to watch. Jane exclaimed to Sarah, "She let him stop short!"

Then Diana went tumbling over the hedge with barely time to put out her hand to break her fall. There was a horrible *crack* in her forearm. It hurt so much that it took Diana's breath away. She couldn't even scream.

"Don't worry, I've got your pony," called Sarah to Diana. She was back on the other side of the hedge, grasping Romilly's reins. "Come on, up you go again. Don't let him think—" She caught sight of Diana's face. "Oh, my goodness!" Jumping off her horse, Sarah bent over Diana. "Are you all right?"

They got Diana to the doctor, and for several weeks afterward her broken arm was in a cast. After her arm healed, she refused to ride. "I don't like Romilly," she said. She'd thought they were friends! How *could* the pony throw her like that? Diana wouldn't even visit the stables to feed him carrots anymore.

Both Sarah and the groom tried to talk Diana into riding again, explaining that everyone fell off sometimes. But Diana's father told her, "Never mind. Don't care much for riding, myself. Give me a good shooting party anytime, eh?"

The following summer, 1970, was a mixture of great fun and awful in-between times. Frances kept her apartment in London, but she and her new husband, Peter Shand Kydd, lived in Sussex now. Diana and Charlie went to visit them at their old farmhouse on the West Sussex coast. Diana's stepfather loved to sail, and he took the children out on his boat.

The midsummer days at Mummy and Peter's stretched on, full of happy, busy things, for hours and hours. At home in Norfolk, even in the summer, Diana and Charlie had to be in bed by eight whether the sun was still up or not. But Peter didn't see any need for children to go to bed before dark, when they didn't have to go to school the next morning.

The bad part of the visit started when it was time for Diana and Charlie to pack their suitcases. Peter talked cheerfully about all the fun they'd have on their next visit. But Frances began crying before Diana and Charlie even left for the train station. "I can't bear to see you go," she sobbed.

Diana hung her head guiltily. Maybe her mother thought she'd *rather* live with her daddy, and that hurt her feelings. Diana hadn't been given a choice, and in fact no one had really explained why all the Spencer children had to stay with their father.

But if Diana had to decide between her parents, which one would she pick? Mummy and Peter would be more fun to live with. But Daddy would be terribly hurt. Besides, Diana would rather stay at Park House, where she'd always lived.

Back at Park House, there would be another unpleasant stage. Daddy always asked about their stay in West Sussex, and at first Diana and Charlie thought he wanted to hear about their good times. But if they said anything more than, "Very nice, Daddy," he would fly into a rage and begin shouting about how their mother spoiled them.

It was better, Diana decided, not to talk to Daddy about Mummy at all.

Back in Norfolk, Sarah and Jane came home from boarding school for their summer holidays. The weather turned very warm, and the children would beg the nanny to take them to the Brancaster beach. Loading a picnic, all their beach gear, and a dog or two into the car, they'd drive through King's Lynn and the few miles farther on to the Spencers' private beach hut. At this point the sea air filled Diana's nostrils, making her wild. She jumped from the car shouting, trying to do everything at once: open up the beach shed and give the dogs water and help Charlie get his pail and shovel out.

That summer the new Disney film, *The Aristocats*, came out. The nanny took them to King's Lynn to see it. Sarah, now fifteen, and Jane, thirteen, felt they were too old for Disney movies, but they had nothing better to do that day. "*The Aristocats*," drawled Sarah in a snooty voice to make the others laugh. "That sounds like a film about the Spencers!"

The movie was about a beautiful white cat named Duchess who belonged to a rich old lady in Paris, France. "The old lady looks a bit like Grandmother Ruth, doesn't she?" remarked Jane. Grandmother Ruth had studied piano at the conservatory in Paris. She was going to be a concert pianist, but then she'd married Grandfather Fermoy instead.

"Mmm," said Sarah. "That cat Duchess reminds me of someone too."

"Shh!" said a woman behind her.

Sarah made a rude face, although not at the woman. After the movie, she explained to her sisters what she'd meant. "Duchess is just like Diana!" she told Jane. "Don't you see it? The way she bats her big blue eyes—the way she fusses over Charlie?"

Jane laughed, nodding. "That's our Duchess, all right."

Diana, holding Charlie's hand, laughed too. She didn't mind her new nickname. Duchess in *The Aristocats* was a beautiful, graceful creature with perfect manners. She had two darling little kittens, a boy and a girl, and she was devoted to them. In the film, a tomcat man-about-town named O'Malley fell in love with her and came to her rescue. "You have eyes like sapphires," said O'Malley to Duchess.

That evening, gazing into the bathroom mirror, Diana murmured, "You have eyes like sapphires."

In late July the big event was the Sandringham Flower Show. They had a special "Fur and Feathers" tent for showing pets, and Diana entered her guinea pig, Peanuts. Her pet won first prize. Diana's father took her picture lying on the grass with Peanuts in front of her. The funny little thing actually was the same color—and the same shape—as a peanut. He was just the right size to fit in Diana's two hands.

But soon after the flower show, the summer took a turn for the worse. As Diana and Charlie were having their breakfast one morning, Johnny Spencer came up the stairs to the nursery. "Well, Diana," he announced, "what do you think? Now that you're nine years old, it's your turn to go off to boarding school."

"What?" Diana paused with her spoonful of oatmeal halfway to her mouth.

"I've enrolled you at Riddlesworth Hall,"

said her father. He looked away from her but went on in a hearty tone. "You'll have ballet lessons and swimming. And your chums are already there: Alexandra Lloyd, and—"

"I don't want to go," said Diana. She looked across the table at her brother, whose lower lip was beginning to tremble. "What about Charlie?" Just the other night he'd had another nightmare about the evil Child Catcher in *Chitty Chitty Bang Bang.* "He'll be so lonely!"

"Nonsense," said her father weakly. "It's only two hours' drive from Park House. You can come home for weekends."

Scrambling out of her chair, Diana put her arms around her brother. "I won't go!" Her voice rose to a scream. "If you love me, you won't make me go!"

"It's all settled," muttered Johnny Spencer. As he hurried out of the nursery, Charlie started to bawl.

When Diana calmed down, she hoped that her mother would take her side. But the next time she visited Frances Shand Kydd, it was at her London apartment. Her mother took her to Harrods, the department store where everyone bought school uniforms. Diana was measured for her gray skirts and blazers. "You'll need gloves and a black bowler hat too," said Frances, "for Sundays at school."

"Mummy, I can't leave Peanuts! What if Marmalade gets him?" Diana's voice quivered.

"But you can take Peanuts with you," said her mother. "The school allows one small pet."

In September, when Sarah and Jane packed to go back to their school, West Heath, Diana packed her trunk for Riddlesworth. Jane came by her room to see how it was going.

"There's no room for my clothes," said Diana. She waved a hand at the piles of white shirts and gray pleated skirts on the bed, all with D. SPENCER labels sewn inside them.

Jane lifted the lid of the new trunk, also marked D. SPENCER. "There'd be plenty of room if you took out your stuffed animals," she said in her sensible way. "They only allow you one 'cuddly' at school, you know."

When Diana arrived at Riddlesworth a few days later, she was assigned to a dormitory. She would sleep in a room with several other girls, each in a narrow metal bed. Diana tucked her fuzzy green hippo under the covers. She'd touched up its eyes with paint that glowed in the dark. That night, Diana lay awake listening to the other homesick girls sobbing. At least Diana had her hippo beside her, looking out for her while she slept.

CHAPTER 4
LOOK AT ME!

After Diana settled in at Riddlesworth Hall, she liked it quite a bit. There was something comforting about going through the same routine, day in and day out. And it was great fun to share a dormitory with other girls her age.

Every night at lights-out, the matron would look in to make sure all the girls were in bed. After she left, Diana would wait a few minutes, then whisper, "Water jump!" The girls popped out of bed and began leaping over the narrow beds. They were pretending to ride horseback in a cross-country competition, with the beds standing in for streams.

Of course it was impossible to play water jump quietly. Before long, a prefect, one of the older girls responsible for keeping the younger ones in order, would appear at their door. "Stop this immediately!" the prefect would bark. That was all part of the fun.

Everyone at school had to have a nickname, and at first some of the girls tried to call Diana "Di." Diana was usually friendly and good-natured, but not when she was called "Di." "Say that again," she told her schoolmates, "and *you* die. I'm Duchess. Duch."

Later in the year, Diana took the part of a Dutch doll in the school play. She was too shy to speak in front of an audience, but the Dutch doll wasn't supposed to say anything. When it was her turn, Diana moved around the stage with stiff movements just like a doll, and everyone clapped for her. Now the nickname "Duch" seemed to fit her even better.

Diana's friends thought it was funny that she liked to eat so much. All of them gobbled the chocolates and biscuits their parents brought on weekend visits, but Diana ate enormous amounts of ordinary food too. "I'll bet you can't eat five pieces of toast," said Alexandra at breakfast one morning.

"No, I can't," said Diana. "I have to eat *six* pieces." And she did. With every slice she wolfed down, the girls at her table laughed harder and harder.

Just as her father had thought, Diana loved the swimming classes at Riddlesworth. In the water, she seemed to turn from a girl into some other creature, like an otter. But dancing was even better—heavenly. Diana decided to become a ballerina when she grew up.

Miss Elizabeth Ridsdale, the headmistress of Riddlesworth Hall, was strict but kind. Diana wasn't the best student, but the teachers praised her for her reading and handwriting. Diana did like to write, especially letters. She wrote dozens of them.

Johnny Spencer had taught Diana to write thank-you letters and get-well letters, and to answer other people's letters right away. Diana liked to please her father, but she also found that letters were a good way to make people happy. The idea wasn't so much to actually *say* anything as to let the other person know you were thinking of him or her.

In fact, sometimes it was better not to say anything. When Diana visited her mother and stepfather that winter, she wrote her father a letter, just as he'd asked her to. But she was careful not to mention the good times she was having with Mummy and Peter. Instead, she wrote that she hoped Daddy was well, and she hoped everyone at Park House was well.

As Diana penned her words in several different colors of ink, she imagined Johnny Spencer at Park House. He would be walking out to check on his herd of cattle, with the dogs trailing behind his Wellington boots. She felt a pang of sadness—she could be with Mummy, or with Daddy, but never with both of them at the same time.

To finish the letter, Diana hoped the weather at Park House was nice. She asked her father to write back. There, that filled up most of the page. Diana signed the letter, then dotted the bottom of the page with X's for kisses and O's for hugs. Now Daddy would know she loved him, and she hadn't said anything about Mummy.

In the spring of 1971, Diana got an especially interesting letter from her father. "Darling Diana," he wrote, "I think you'll like the new nanny. Her name is Mary Clarke. Charlie is fond of her already. she'll pick you up at the end of term."

Diana wasn't so sure she'd like the new nanny. But when July came and Mary Clarke appeared at Riddlesworth, Diana found out her father was right. During the two-hour ride to Park House, Diana chattered about her friends at school and Peanuts and dancing and swimming.

At the mention of swimming, Miss Clarke smiled. "There's a surprise waiting for you at home. No, I can't tell you what it is, or it wouldn't be a surprise, would it?"

Johnny Spencer met them on the front

drive of Park House. He insisted on leading Diana around to the back of the house, before she even went inside. They crossed the back lawn and walked around the fenced tennis court.

"It's a camel—I know it's a camel," Diana teased her father. He had the same excited, triumphant look on his face as when he'd brought Bert the camel to her seventh birthday.

Then Diana stopped and gasped. "Oh, Daddy!" The last time she was home there had been only grass and shrubs between the tennis court and the edge of the Sandringham parkland. Now, blue water sparkled there. "A swimming pool!" It was a beautiful big pool with *two* diving boards and a slide.

"I had the pool built with a heater," said Johnny Spencer proudly, "so you can swim anytime."

Anytime, every time! That day Diana swam before lunch, and then she swam all afternoon until dinnertime. Over and over she practiced the dives she'd learned at school. Although all the family enjoyed the pool, Diana loved it the best. It was a popular place for the Spencers' friends, too. On hot August days anyone might show up to swim, including Prince Andrew and Prince Edward.

Johnny Spencer took dozens of pictures of Diana diving. He made a safety rule that you couldn't dive from the slide, but Diana couldn't resist. It was so exciting to be really good at something, for a change. She ran to the top of the slide, calling out, "Look at me!" When they were all looking she'd push off from the slide, arc through the air, and slip into the water with perfectly straight legs.

Sarah, now sixteen, was almost as delighted with the pool as Diana was. But she was out on horseback almost every day as well. Sarah was good at *everything:* swimming, riding, playing the piano. She was pretty, and her lively personality seemed to go with her bright red hair. Everyone called her "Ginge," short for "Ginger."

Ginge knew a lot about boys. "Boys don't

like fat girls," she warned Diana. Diana paused, wide-eyed, halfway through a bowl of bread pudding. She finished it, anyway, but it didn't taste as good.

That summer Diana thought she might have been too hasty, giving up riding. If she rode, she could spend more time with Sarah—maybe even be a little bit like her. So Diana tried riding once more. But this time her pony stepped in a rabbit hole and stumbled, and she fell off again. She didn't break anything, but she gave up riding for good.

The next spring, 1972, Diana saw Grandmother Cynthia for the last time. Johnny Spencer took Diana and Charlie to Althorp for the spring holidays. Their father seemed glum and sad during the visit, but Diana thought it was only that he hated being in the same house with Grandfather Spencer.

On the rainy days of the visit, Diana and Charlie explored the attics of Althorp. They tried on funny old clothes from bygone years and giggled over funny old objects, like a chamber pot painted with roses. "I'll bet it didn't *smell* like roses," said Charlie. They discovered piles of photograph albums, and they brought some of them downstairs to show Grandmother Cynthia.

They had tea in Grandmother Cynthia's sitting room, decorated in a soft blue with delicate flowers. Diana's grandmother didn't seem quite herself. Diana and Charlie often had to repeat their questions. But when she poured out at tea, she remembered exactly how each of them liked their tea. Two lumps of sugar for Charlie, and three for Diana. The little watercress sandwiches on the tea table were cut into stars and crescent moons.

And Grandmother Cynthia's blue eyes shone as Diana told her about her life at boarding school. "You were awarded the Legatt Cup for helpfulness! My dear, I am so proud of you. This is what it means to be of noble blood. Never forget that you are a Spencer."

Remembering this conversation later,

Diana realized that Grandmother Cynthia must never have forgotten that *she* was the daughter of the Duke of Abercorn. Knowing your proud heritage, thought Diana, didn't mean lording it over other people. It meant that, since you were noble, you ought to behave nobly. And it meant that there was always something solid behind you when life was hardest.

Charlie opened one of the albums they'd found in the attic, and the three of them pored over the old pictures. "Now, this"—Grandmother Cynthia paused to smile—"this is your grandfather and myself on our wedding day in nineteen nineteen. Dear me, it seems like yesterday—but it was all of thirty-one years ago."

Charlie, always quick at arithmetic, gave Diana a worried glance. Even Diana could work out in her head that 1972 minus 1919 did not equal 31. Grandmother Cynthia ought to know that too.

Diana and Charlie were right to think

something was wrong. Next autumn the sad news came that Grandmother Cynthia had died of a brain tumor. Johnny Spencer took the children to London for the memorial service at the Chapel Royal in St. James's Palace. In this very church Queen Victoria had married Prince Albert in 1840. It was an honor befitting the noble lineage of the Spencers that the service for Cynthia, Countess Spencer, was held here. The Queen Mother and Princess Margaret attended, as well as other important guests.

But Diana didn't care about the honor. Tears ran down her face throughout the liturgy. As the soprano voices of the boys' choir soared in the last hymn, she began to sob out loud. Grandfather Spencer leaned over from his end of the pew to glare at Diana, but she couldn't stop.

That same year, 1972, Frances and Peter Shand Kydd moved all the way to Scotland. Diana's mother now lived hundreds of miles from Norfolk. She wasn't even in a part of Scotland that was convenient to get to, like Edinburgh. The Shand Kydds moved to a sheep farm on the out-of-the way Isle of Seil, on the west coast. Frances wouldn't be able to visit Diana at school on weekends, and Diana couldn't visit her mother and stepfather often either.

Diana didn't talk to Johnny Spencer about the way she felt, but one afternoon between swims she talked to Mary Clarke. "I'll never ever marry unless I really love, *really love*, someone," said Diana. She paused, gazing into the wavelets of the swimming pool. She could almost see her future children's faces in the blue water. There were four, or maybe six, dear little boys and girls gazing back at her. "If you're not really sure you love someone," Diana went on, "then you might get divorced. I never want to be divorced!"

CHAPTER 5
TRUE LOVE

During Diana's last year at Riddlesworth, she discovered the most wonderful books. They were written by Barbara Cartland, and they were all about love. The story might take place in England early in the nineteenth century, or in Germany before World War I, or in an imaginary European country during the reign of Queen Victoria. But it was always the same fascinating story.

First, a young woman meets an older, sophisticated man. In the middle chapters, he rescues her once or twice, maybe from bandits, or from a whirlpool—even from a mean husband. Gazing at the heroine, the hero feels something he has never felt before, although he has known many women. Finally, the man and the young woman declare their love for each other. The flames of passion (true love always felt like flames, it seemed) consume them. And that was the very satisfying end.

Diana quickly read all the romance novels circulating around her dormitory. She bought some of her own to add to the pool. Luckily there seemed to be no end to them.

Meanwhile that autumn, 1972, Diana's personal heroine, "Ginge," suddenly ended her studies at West Heath. At first Diana heard only that Daddy and Grandmother Ruth had decided to send Sarah to a finishing school in Switzerland. After that, they enrolled her at a conservatory in Vienna.

Diana thought that made sense: Sarah, talented at the piano but careless with academic studies, should study music full time. But later Diana heard the real story from Jane: Sarah had been caught drunk at West Heath, and the headmistress, Ruth Rudge, had expelled her in disgrace.

The next time Diana saw Sarah, though, her

oldest sister explained it a different way. "Miss Rudge wanted to know why I would drink vodka at school." Sarah rolled her eyes, as if the answer were obvious. "Sheer boredom, my dear Rudge!" Whatever flame-haired "Ginge" did, she managed to make it seem dashing.

In the spring, Sarah turned eighteen. Johnny Spencer threw a magnificent coming-out party for her. The setting was a Norman castle, Castle Rising, in Norfolk. Johnny hired horse-drawn carriages to bring the guests to the castle, along a path lit by real torches. The Spencer girls noticed that their father had a date, Countess Dartmouth, for the party. But with all the excitement about Sarah, they didn't think much about it.

The next time Diana and her sisters came home for a weekend, their father surprised them all at breakfast. "I've invited a good friend for luncheon. Her name is Raine, Lady Dartmouth. I do hope you'll like her as much as I do."

As soon as Johnny Spencer left the room,

Sarah gave a dry laugh. "I doubt that very much, Father dear."

Jane sighed. "I suppose Daddy thinks he's found true love."

"How do you know he's in love with her?" asked Diana. "He only said she was a good friend." Her sisters looked pityingly at her.

Nanny Mary Clarke said they were supposed to dress up for the luncheon, so Diana put on her Riddlesworth dark red jacket and gray skirt. Charlie also wore his school uniform. When Diana came down to the drawing room at noontime, her father was wearing a suit and tie.

Sarah, however, slouched into the room in jeans and a sweater. Johnny Spencer frowned and started to speak, but just then the butler opened the drawing room door. "Lady Dartmouth," he announced.

"Oh, my lord," muttered Sarah, just loud enough for Diana to hear.

Their father's "good friend" swept into the room draped in floral chiffon. An enormous diamond pin glittered on the front of her dress. Raine, Lady Dartmouth, wore her shoulder-length hair curled and puffed, and sprayed to stay that way. Bright lipstick set off her ferocious smile and matched the polish on her fingernails.

"Johnny, how *lovely* of you to have me!" She turned her face for a kiss on the cheek. "And your dear girls—" She shook hands with Jane, the nearest, then with Diana. "And Sarah, your debutante"—Raine's glance paused just for an instant on Sarah's jeans, and then she turned quickly, her chiffon floating behind, to Charlie—"and Charles, the son and heir!" Her eyes flicked over Mary Clarke, and she nodded to the nanny.

Jane and Diana smiled weakly, while Charlie and Sarah didn't smile at all. But Johnny Spencer didn't seem to notice. Beaming at Raine, he offered his arm. "Shall we go to luncheon?"

"Delighted," purred Raine, looking into his eyes. The two of them led the way into the dining room. Behind their backs, Sarah pretended to stick a finger down her throat.

Diana sat down at the table with her stomach in a knot. Would Sarah say something outright rude to Raine? Daddy would be so upset.

At the same time, Diana was disgusted with her father. Sarah and Jane were right: anyone could see that he thought he was in love. How could he fall for Raine after having been married to a naturally elegant lady like Mummy?

As the soup was served, Lady Dartmouth kept up a bright chatter. The diamonds in her pin flashed as she turned from one side of the table to the other, tossing out questions and remarks. But Johnny Spencer had to answer the questions she asked the children. They only muttered "yes" or "no" at their soup plates. Mary Clarke tried to move the conversation along by remarking on the weather, but the strain grew tighter and tighter.

Still smiling brightly, Raine asked Sarah one more question. Diana felt so tense, she could hardly sit still. Then Sarah put down her silver soup spoon, gazed sincerely into Raine's face—and gave a loud belch.

There was a shocked silence, in which Raine's smile froze. Then Johnny Spencer's face turned red. "Sarah. Leave the table at once."

Sarah left, and Diana loyally followed. In Sarah's room, Sarah gave her younger sister a hug. She giggled. "Raine, Raine, go away—"

Diana joined in, "*Don't* come again some other day!" Sarah took a bag of Twiglets, crunchy pretzel-like sticks, from her closet. They stretched out on the bed to enjoy their private luncheon.

In September 1973, Diana started at her sisters' boarding school, West Heath. Sarah had left in disgrace last year, of course, but Jane was still there. Jane was an excellent student, and she'd also been chosen as a prefect.

As Diana arranged her things in the ten-bed dormitory, the girl assigned to the next bed came over to chat. "I'm Carolyn Pride. I've got toffee in my tuck box, if you want some."

Carolyn waved a hand at the pictures on the walls. "Look, they've given us the whole royal family."

Glancing at the wall above her bed, Diana giggled. "And *I've* got Prince Charles! Lucky me." It was a photo of him in his ermine cape and gold coronet, at his investiture as Prince of Wales.

"The *Daily Mail* had a picture of him with Lady Jane Wellesley," Carolyn went on. "I think he should marry her, don't you? She's so pretty, and her father's the Duke of Wellington. What more does he want?"

"True love," said Diana. "By the way, do you like Barbara Cartland books?"

Carolyn did, and so did the other friends they made at West Heath. They exchanged their private stashes of romances and read the books during study periods and in bed late at night.

At West Heath, Diana was on the swim team, as she had been at Riddlesworth, and she won prizes for swimming and diving. Her teammates were in awe of her dive that they called the "Spencer Special," in which she slipped into the water as easily as a kingfisher. Again, Diana took piano and dance lessons. She threw herself into ballet, even though the ballet teacher said she could never become a ballerina. At the age of twelve, Diana was already five feet ten inches.

"You see," the teacher explained kindly, "the art of ballet is all about creating exquisitely beautiful scenes on the stage. A ballerina taller than her male dancing partner—" The teacher gave a rueful shrug. Diana nodded miserably, hunching her shoulders.

After a while, Diana was comforted by the thought that she could still become a ballet *teacher*. That would be great fun, teaching little girls who wanted to become ballerinas. In any case, she never thought of giving up dancing. Dancing was like swimming, only she was swimming in the music instead of in the water. On nights when Diana couldn't sleep, she sneaked into the dance room. Turning on the music very low, she twirled and leaped through her routines until she was exhausted.

Diana soon made friends with the matron at West Heath, Violet Allen, who looked after the girls in the dormitories. Miss. Allen also ran the infirmary, where Diana sometimes came to get some medicine for an upset stomach. "Too much chocolate," said Miss Allen, but she didn't scold. Diana got in the habit of coming to the matron just because she needed a hug, or to help her tidy up. It was so satisfying to bustle around with a broom and dustpan and turn a messy room into a spick-and-span room. It was even more satisfying to hear Violet Allen say, "Diana, dear, what would I *do* without you?"

The headmistress at West Heath, Ruth Rudge, aimed to instill "character and confidence" in her students. Besides their studies and sports, all the girls were expected to do social work. With several other girls Diana volunteered to go to Darenth Park, a hospital for the handicapped and mentally disabled.

As the West Heath minibus pulled up in

front of the huge Victorian building for the first time, the girl next to Diana shuddered. "Ugh, creepy," she whispered.

Inside the hospital, Muriel Stevens, who organized the visits, instructed the girls, "Now, some of the patients may look very odd to you, and they may act oddly, but try not to move away from them. Get down on their level, if they're in a wheelchair. And let them touch you." She smiled reassuringly. "They won't bite!"

The hospital had arranged a dance, and music was playing in the big room when Miss Stevens ushered the girls in. Diana's heart went out to the patients. Of course they wouldn't bite—for one thing, many of them seemed to have lost their teeth. Stooping in front of a wheelchair, Diana smiled at the girl in it. Her name, Rose, was pinned to the front of her blouse.

"Hello, Rose. I'm Diana." Rose seemed to be older than Diana, but the look in her eyes was as clueless as a baby's. With a gesture like a baby's, she reached out to pat Diana's face.

"Would you like to dance, Rose?" asked Diana. "They're playing our song!" Miss Allen had explained how to "dance" with the wheelchair patients by pushing them in time to the music. But Diana had a better idea. Facing Rose and grasping the wheelchair arms, she began to dance backward. "Hold on! La, la, la-la!" Rose laughed in delight, showing her toothless gums.

Diana swung Rose around and around the hall in graceful swoops. The song ended, and she went on to another patient, and then another. As she danced, Diana began to notice that she was the only West Heath girl who seemed to be having fun. Never mind; the patients were smiling and laughing, and so were the nurses.

During Diana's years at West Heath, she and her sisters kept hoping that Raine would indeed go away. But every time they came home to Park House, there was some further

CHAPTER 6

LADY DIANA

One evening in June 1975, Diana was in her dormitory at West Heath, having a nice long soak in the bath. On the rack across the bathtub she'd propped up *The Wild Unwilling Wife,* by Barbara Cartland. The steamy mist of the bathroom made it seem almost probable that the timid, childlike heroine could save the man she loved by shooting a charging lion.

A knock on the bathroom door interrupted Diana's romance trance. "Duch," said one of her dormitory mates, "you've got a call. It's important."

Diana hastily dried herself off, wrapped her wet hair in a towel, and hurried to the phone. It was her father. Grandfather Spencer had just died.

Johnny Spencer didn't sound very sorry, and Diana couldn't feel too sad either. Grandfather Spencer was eighty-three, and he'd been unhappy ever since Grandmother Cynthia died. He'd never seemed interested in Diana—or even in her father, his own son and heir, for that matter.

Still, Grandfather Spencer's passing meant a big change for them. Diana's father was now the eighth Earl Spencer. Charlie's new title was Viscount Althorp, and Diana and her sisters became Lady Sarah, Lady Jane, and—Lady Diana.

"I'm a lady!" shrieked Diana, running down the hall. Her bathrobe flapped around her. Heads popped out of doors, laughing. Carolyn gave her a mock curtsy.

When Diana calmed down, though, she realized the truly sad part of this news. The Spencers would leave Park House, which they had only leased from the royal family, and move to Althorp. Great, gloomy Althorp, without Grandmother Spencer to soften it.

Besides, Park House had been Diana's home ever since she was born! Charlie felt the same way. Back at Park House for the summer holidays, they had to step around boxes and crates. "That's the chair you booby-trapped for Nanny," said Diana, watching a servant carry it down the stairs.

Charlie smiled wistfully. "Didn't she jump when she sat on the pin?"

What made it worse was that Raine, Countess Dartmouth, seemed to be in charge of the packing. She swept up and down the stairs, beckoning to the servants in her grandest way, giving orders right and left. "I don't know what I'd do without your help," Johnny told Raine.

"I do," muttered Diana to Charlie. The two of them wandered through the emptying house. Even the laundry room, where Diana had washed and ironed so many of Sarah's clothes, seemed like a very dear place.

In the nearby kitchen, Elsie, the cook, was gloomy too. She and her husband, Bertie Betts, were losing their jobs. Still, the kitchen was full of the comforting smell of chocolate cake. "Oh, Elsie!" Diana hugged the cook. "My favorite, with buttercream icing." Tears ran down her face as she dug into a big wedge of cake.

After a long swim in the pool, Diana felt calmer.

But the first time Diana came "home" to Althorp, she was upset all over again. She hadn't visited Althorp for three years, since Grandmother Cynthia's death. Althorp House was even bigger and grayer than she'd remembered.

Diana stood beside her father in the entrance hall, gazing up at the gallery where all the portraits hung. She frowned. There seemed to be some gaps among the rows of paintings.

"Diana, dear!" Raine, Lady Dartmouth, dressed in a cashmere sweater set and pearls, appeared at the top of the stairs. "I can't wait to show you your room. I know you'll adore it— furniture all in white, so suitable for a young lady. And you have a *stunning* view of the rear gardens, with the lily pond."

Johnny Spencer beamed at Raine. "You have the feminine touch—a real flair for decorating."

Without responding to Raine, Diana ran up the stairs to the portrait gallery. There was one particular painting she wanted to see. It was the portrait of Grandmother Cynthia when she was the young Countess Spencer, only a few years older than fourteen-year-old Diana. Grandmother Cynthia's eyes, the same clear blue that Diana remembered, seemed to gaze lovingly down on her granddaughter. Diana breathed a sigh.

As she moved around the gallery, Diana began to realize which paintings were missing. Two by the famous artist Van Dyck, for instance. When Diana asked her father, he admitted that they had been sold. "I haven't wanted to bother you or Charlie and your sisters about the finances," he explained, "but the death duties on your grandfather's estate amounted to *four million pounds*. The Van Dycks fetched me a million each."

"Was it Raine's idea to sell them?" Diana asked innocently.

"Yes, she's been an enormous help, talking with art dealers and so on. I wouldn't know where to begin."

Johnny Spencer talked as if Raine were only "visiting" and "consulting," but to the Spencer children it was clear that she had moved in. She occupied the grand India Silk Bedroom.

One weekend at Althorp, Diana was idly flipping through one of her father's magazines, the *Field*, when an envelope dropped out. It was a letter addressed to Viscount Althorp in Raine's handwriting. Diana eased the letter out of the envelope and read it. Mushy stuff at the beginning, and then—

Diana felt sick. Raine had written Johnny pages of advice about redecorating Althorp House. Diana indignantly turned back to the first page to check the date. Why, Raine had written this before Grandfather Spencer died! What a vulture!

The first weekend that Sarah and Jane came

home, the three sisters managed to corner Johnny Spencer alone. "Daddy, it's not that we don't want you to get married again," said Sarah. Jane added, so that there would be no misunderstanding, "Just make it anyone but Raine." Diana nodded, pleading silently with her eyes. Johnny Spencer laughed uncomfortably, but at least he didn't say it was none of their business.

Sarah and Jane didn't come home often, and it was lonely at Althorp for Diana and Charlie. They missed the friends they'd grown up with, the boys and girls who used to drop by Park House to play tennis or swim in the pool.

"Do you know," Charlie informed his sister, "that Althorp is as big as the country of Monaco?"

"No wonder it seems like the middle of nowhere," sighed Diana. She knew something about the tiny country of Monaco, mainly because Grace Kelly, the film star of the 1950s, had married Prince Ranier III of Monaco. Their daughter, Princess Caroline, was Jane's age, and was sometimes gossiped about as a suitable bride for Prince Charles.

At Althorp House, Diana quickly made friends with the servants, especially the cook. Upstairs at lunch or dinner with her father and Raine, she hardly said anything. Downstairs in the kitchen, she chattered easily. Sometimes she even baked a dessert, like bread pudding, for the servants.

Before long, Raine wasn't Countess Dartmouth anymore. In the spring of 1976 her husband, Lord Dartmouth, divorced her. The Spencer children could see what was coming. "If you marry that woman," Sarah warned Johnny Spencer, "we wash our hands of you."

But it was no use. In July, Johnny and Raine were married in a private ceremony in London. Johnny Spencer notified Miss Rudge, as well as the headmaster of Charlie's school, and let them inform Diana and Charlie: Raine was now Countess Spencer.

Hearing the news, Diana flung herself on her bed and sobbed. "The dragon lady's got my father!" she told Carolyn. "They're on their *honeymoon*. Nothing will ever be the same again."

Much as Diana disliked her stepmother, she liked one thing about her very much: That was Raine's mother, Barbara Cartland. The famous romance novelist was now Diana's stepgrandmother.

The first time Barbara came to Althorp to visit Raine, Diana was thrilled. While Raine with her theatrical aristocratic airs offended Diana, Barbara Cartland delighted her. Maybe it was that Raine looked so annoyed at the sight of her mother, stepping out of her white Rolls-Royce in a pink chiffon gown and black false eyelashes. She held out a stack of books tied with a pink silk bow. "These are for you, Diana—a little bird told me you enjoy my books."

At lunchtime, Diana listened fascinated to Barbara's conversation. Diana noticed with amazement that Barbara's voice was breathless and girlish, just like the heroines in her romance novels. Barbara Cartland heroines said things like, "When I am close to you I feel safe . . . and so very . . . very . . . happy."

Of course, what Barbara said in her breathy voice was not so meek. "They *will* talk about me," she told Johnny Spencer, "but I will never be a . . . modest little flower doing my bit in a corner. I am a . . . whirlwind."

Raine, Countess Spencer, gave her mother a sour look. Diana smiled down at her plate. A pink whirlwind for a mother was just what Raine deserved.

CHAPTER 7

THICK AS A PLANK

"You're Jane Spencer's sister, aren't you?" the teachers at West Heath always asked. Diana blushed and nodded, but she wished they wouldn't make the connection. Jane, like Charlie, was terribly clever. Now in her last year at West Heath, Jane had passed eleven O levels, the nation-wide exams for sixteen-year-olds, with flying colors. Jane had also been sensible, dependable, and captain of the lacrosse team. Everyone—students, teachers, Miss Rudge—liked and admired Jane Spencer.

Diana was good at sports, like her sisters. She won trophies in swimming and diving all four years at West Heath. But in the classroom, she couldn't seem to concentrate. As soon as the teacher began talking about the principal rivers of India, or quadratic equations, a film would switch on in Diana's mind.

The heroine of the film was always Diana, except that she was five inches shorter. And instead of the school uniform, she was wearing a trailing velvet gown. A tall, handsome man of the world put a finger under her chin to tilt her face up. "Your eyes are like sapphires," he murmured as he bent to kiss her.

"Which is what—Miss Spencer?" Diana came out of her daydream to realize that the teacher was asking her a question. But she was dazed, not even sure which class she was in. Should the answer be something like, "The Ganges River flows from the Himalayas to the Bay of Bengal," or a mathematical formula?

The only subject Diana could concentrate on was English history, the parts about the kings and queens and lords and ladies. English history was also Spencer family history, and Diana knew it from strolling around the portrait gallery at Althorp.

There was Georgiana, secretly married to

John Spencer at the age of sixteen. She had become a brilliant hostess, famous for her high-stakes gambling parties at Althorp. There was Sarah Jennings, Duchess of Marlborough, whose beautiful daughter was also named Diana Spencer. The duchess had schemed to marry that Diana to the Prince of Wales, son of King George II. Stories like these blended easily with the romance novels Diana read, and she remembered them without trying.

In spite of her pride in her aristocratic family, Diana didn't like going home to Althorp. Raine was always there, firmly in charge of Diana's father and his estate. One of Raine's moneymaking projects was to turn the Althorp estate into a tourist attraction. The grand old stables, the most beautiful building on the estate, had been turned into a gift shop and tea-room. Raine herself ran the shop and sold tickets for tours of Althorp House, and the eighth Earl Spencer cheerfully led tours.

Diana wished she could refuse to visit Althorp at all. That was Sarah's policy, and it was all right for *her*. She was out of school, so she could go off to South Africa for a months-long vacation. By 1977, Sarah was working and living on her own in London.

Sometimes Diana visited Sarah on weekends. She came away from these visits excited but troubled. Sarah's life in London seemed so glamorous! On the other hand, something was wrong with Sarah. She was so thin that Diana could count her ribs. Sarah pretended to eat, but she hardly ate anything. When the sisters went shopping, she was delighted to fit into tinier and tinier dresses.

At Althorp, to get away from Raine and all her hateful changes, Diana would go to the lake at the back of the grounds and row out to the island. It was only a little island, just big enough for one. Diana had it all to herself. On warm days she could lie in the sun, read, and pretend she was somewhere far away from Althorp.

In the spring of 1977, the girls in Diana's class at West Heath faced the O-level exams coming up in June. They were either studying for O levels or avoiding studying for O levels. One of the ways they avoided was by sitting around the dormitory munching Twiglets, reading the tabloid papers, and gossiping. "Ooh, now Action Man is dating Princess Caroline of Monaco! Watch out, Diana."

"Action Man" was the media's name for Prince Charles. He had trained in the Royal Air Force (RAF) as a fighter pilot, and now he was an officer in the Royal Navy. He loved playing polo and riding to the hunt, both rather risky sports.

Glancing at the portrait of Charles over her bed, Diana smiled. "Don't be silly. He'll never marry her. She's Catholic." When Charles became King of England, he would also be the head of the Protestant Anglican Church. So it would not do for his wife to be Catholic. This rule was actually written in British law. As heir to the British throne, he could not marry a divorced woman, either. He could not marry at all without the consent of the queen or

Parliament, the lawmaking body of the British government.

Diana's friends were so nervous about the exams. They stalked around the halls saying things like, "Help! I'll never get the quadratic equation straight!" The night before, the head-mistress visited them and gave them aspirin.

But Diana didn't feel nervous. She didn't feel, or think, anything about the O levels. In her mind they were like a fence that she was supposed to jump her pony over. If she didn't ride, she wouldn't have to jump, would she? When Diana sat down with the exam book, her mind was perfectly blank.

Diana took her O levels in June, and she failed all five exams, one after the other: English language, geography, art, history, and English literature. "I don't understand this, Diana," said her English teacher. "In my class, you wrote a very perceptive paper on Jane Austen's novels. Why didn't you write like that on the exam?" The history teacher said much the same thing about the history exam. "You know English history backwards and forwards! How could you fail?"

Diana didn't know the answer. She ducked her head and shrugged. "I guess I'm just as thick as a plank." Even Sarah, who'd spent her time at West Heath drinking and getting into scrapes, had passed six O levels.

"What does it matter?" Carolyn tried to comfort her. "We're all just going to get married, anyway. It's not as if you wanted to go to Oxford." But Diana knew that even to get a decent job, the kind of job she might like to have while she waited to get married, you needed to pass a few O levels. She would have to try again in December.

While Diana was busy failing her exams, her sister Sarah was busy with a new boyfriend. She'd been invited to Ascot week, the house party at Windsor Castle, where the royal family watched the world-famous Royal Ascot races every June. Prince Charles had been taken with pretty, lively, horse-loving Sarah Spencer. He invited her to watch him play polo in a match at Windsor.

Diana's friends at West Heath peppered her with questions about her sister and Prince Charles. "Does she really have to call him 'sir'?"; "Is he in love with her?"; "Does she mind about his other girlfriends?"

At Althorp, Raine was thrilled that the Prince of Wales was interested in her step-daughter, in spite of the fact that Sarah never said a polite word to her. "Imagine—the most eligible bachelor in the world, sweet on our Sarah! We must throw a *splendid* hunt ball at Althorp this autumn."

Johnny Spencer also seemed proud that his daughter was dating Prince Charles. Johnny and Raine planned a shooting party on the estate and a ball at Althorp House in November 1977, and they invited Prince Charles for that weekend. To the Spencers' delight, he accepted.

CHAPTER 8
PRINCE CHARMING

Diana came home from West Heath for the weekend of the ball, greatly excited at the thought of rubbing elbows with Sarah's sophisticated friends. The shooting party was for men only and, anyway, Diana didn't want to kill anything. But it was the custom for the girls and women to take a picnic lunch out to the men. Diana, dressed in a checked shirt, corduroy pants, and Wellington boots, cheerfully joined in.

Diana was in high spirits, talking and laughing, as happy to be at the party as the hunting dogs were. During the picnic, Prince Charles, followed by his black Labrador retriever, Harvey, came over to meet Diana, and she curtsied to him. That was proper, but it seemed funny to be curtsying while wearing Wellington boots. Giggling, Diana also made a curtsy to Charles's dog. Charles laughed, and Harvey, wagging his tail, seemed to laugh too.

At that moment, Sarah appeared and took the prince's arm. "Sir, did you meet my little sister? *Isn't* Diana a dear? She does all my laundry when I'm home." With a trilling laugh, Sarah pulled Charles away.

The night of the ball, Diana wore her first real evening gown. It was dotted organza, the same color blue as her eyes. She wore the gold chain and heart that her father had given her in July for her sixteenth birthday. Prince Charles asked her to dance, whirling her around and around the hall. He seemed to like her, Diana—could that be true? Diana, who was too tall and too pudgy, not as witty or daring as Sarah?

As the song ended Charles asked, "Will you show me the gallery? I hear there are some Joshua Reynolds portraits in the collection."

"Yes . . . there are," said Diana, ducking her

head and blushing. She started to lead him toward the main staircase.

But just then Sarah swept toward them. "Sir, you must think I'm a dreadful hostess!" she exclaimed to Prince Charles. "I *promised* to show you the gallery." She smiled a little too sweetly at her sister. "Thank you so much just the same, Duch."

Diana gave her sister a sweet smile in return. "At least let me tell you where the light switches for the gallery are. You wouldn't know."

That night after the ball, Diana drifted dreamily around her room, remembering what it had been like to dance with Charles, Prince of Wales. He was a little taller than she was. He seemed to like putting his arm around her waist. And . . . there was something wistful about him, something that made Diana want to cheer him up.

In December, Diana took her O-level exams again. Again, she failed them all. She had to leave West Heath.

When Diana's mother heard about the exam results, she sighed. "I think the answer is the Institut Alpin Videmanette," she said. That was the finishing school where Sarah had gone after her disgrace at West Heath.

"I can't go there," protested Diana. "Sarah says they make you speak French all the time. Your roommates aren't even allowed to speak to you in English."

"Diana, the whole point is to learn French!" laughed her mother. "Sarah was fluent in six weeks."

So after Christmas, Diana went off to finishing school in Switzerland. This school was nothing like her jolly life at West Heath. The other girls, very chic and international, ignored her as they jabbered away in French. Since Diana wasn't allowed to speak English, she didn't say anything.

Almost every day Diana wrote her mother, or her father, or both of them. "I hate this beastly place! Please, please let me come home. You're wasting your money! They teach you to cook everything with gobs of cream and butter, and I'm growing out of my clothes. I hate, hate everything about Institut Alpin Videmanette!"

This last sentence wasn't strictly true. Since the school was in the Swiss Alps, the girls went skiing every day. Diana quickly learned to swoop around the slopes. For a few hours she was free under the bright blue sky, breathing fresh air and showing that she was a good athlete, even if she was thick as a plank.

During February 1978, the other students suddenly became interested in Diana. Sarah Spencer's name was in the international society news. She was vacationing at Klosters, a Swiss ski resort, with Prince Charles. All the gossip columnists wanted to know if Lady Sarah Spencer was on her way to becoming Princess of Wales and the future Queen Sarah. The students at Videmanette wanted to know, too, and they eagerly questioned Diana about her sister's romance with the prince. But Diana still couldn't speak enough French to tell them much, and they soon gave up.

In April, Diana's parents gave up on the finishing school and let her come home to England. Jane was getting married to Robert Fellowes, the queen's assistant private secretary. It seemed to Diana that her father and Grandmother Ruth were glad Jane would be connected with the royal court, but a little disappointed that she hadn't even tried to marry into the royal family itself.

Diana was happy to be home and to be her sister's maid of honor. But the wedding day was marred, at least for Diana, by the bad feelings between Frances Shand Kydd and Johnny and Raine Spencer. Naturally there had to be one picture of Jane, the bride, with just her mother and father. But when Raine was asked to step out of the picture, she made a fuss.

After Jane's wedding, Diana wasn't sure where to live or what to do. She certainly didn't want to live at Althorp with her father and Raine. She would have liked to live on her own in London, but her mother and father thought she was too young, at sixteen. Diana would have been delighted to live with Sarah and her roommate, but Sarah didn't think that was a good idea.

For a few months Diana worked as a nanny for family friends in Hampshire. Then she moved into her mother's apartment in London. She took jobs here and there, taking care of children and cleaning houses. Since Diana hadn't passed her O-level exams, she wasn't qualified for anything else. But she liked cleaning house and looking after children, and these jobs left her plenty of time for fun.

One weekend in September 1978, Diana was staying with her friend Caroline Harbord-Hammond at her family's house in Norfolk. Out of the blue, she had a sudden premonition about her father. "My father is going to drop down," she blurted out.

Her hostess looked startled. "Whatever do you mean?"

Diana blushed and shook her head. "I don't know why—I just had a feeling." Suddenly she was on the point of tears, and her hostess tact-fully changed the subject.

The next day, there was a telephone call for Diana: Johnny Spencer had suffered a cerebral hemorrhage. He was in the hospital, and he was not expected to live.

Diana and her sisters and brother rushed to Northampton General Hospital, where their father barely clung to life for two days. Then there seemed to be some hope. Raine had Johnny moved to London, where he could get the best medical care.

During the next three months, the eighth Earl Spencer lay in the hospital, and Raine practically lived there with him. Diana, Charlie, and their sisters were shocked to discover that Raine would not allow them to see their father. "Johnny's life is at stake," declared Countess Spencer. "I will *not* allow any nega-tive influence near him."

Sarah and Charlie lost their tempers and shouted at their stepmother in the hospital cor-ridor. Diana hung around the hospital room, nibbling chocolate and waiting for a chance to see her father. Whenever Raine left, Diana and the others sneaked into his room. But Johnny Spencer was unconscious much of the time. Even when he was awake, he couldn't talk, since he had a tube in his throat.

Meanwhile, Sarah's romance with Prince Charles didn't seem to be going anywhere. After the skiing trip with him last spring, she'd given an interview to a reporter about her relationship with the prince. "If Prince Charles asked me to marry him, I would turn him down." That quotation made headlines in the tabloid papers, of course. Diana's opinion was that Sarah *did* want to marry the prince. But now she'd never have the chance.

Besides the fascinating subject of whom Prince Charles might or might not marry, the tabloid headlines were also buzzing about a royal marriage on the rocks. Princess Margaret, Queen Elizabeth's younger sister, was divorcing her husband of eighteen years, Antony Armstrong-Jones. Princess Margaret had had to get the queen's permission to marry him, and now she'd had to get her permission to divorce him.

In November, both Sarah and Diana were invited to a party at Buckingham Palace in honor of Prince Charles's thirtieth birthday. There would be hundreds of other guests, but still, the invitation was an honor. "Would you mind if I accepted?" Diana asked her sister.

Sarah frowned, then shrugged. "If you want to. What would you wear, though?" She laughed. "You can't wear one of your loose Laura Ashley frocks, you know. And you don't have anything suitable for evening."

"I've got the dress I wore to Jane's engagement party," said Diana.

"Does it still fit you?" asked Sarah. "I'd let you borrow something of mine, but . . ."

"But I'd have to stitch two of your dresses together to make one for me, is that it?" asked Diana with a resentful laugh. "I'll lose weight." She was hurt by the way her sister talked about her. Sarah always had to win, no matter what.

She thought she could be the best at everything, even at losing weight.

By starving herself, Diana did lose enough weight to wear her dress. At the party, Prince Charles only spoke to her once, as she entered the palace with Sarah and Sarah's date. Charles's own date was Susan George, a movie actress. But Diana was thrilled just to be at Buckingham Palace, at the prince's birthday party.

Early in 1979, Johnny Spencer was well enough to come home to Althorp, although he was still feeble and had trouble talking. Diana had to admit that Raine had pulled him through. Raine had hardly left his bedside all those weeks. She'd done everything possible to make her husband get well, from getting experimental medication, to calling in an exorcist, to preventing his own children from bothering him.

Earl Spencer had been in love with Raine before his illness, but now he clearly thought she could do no wrong. Besides selling some of the finest art in the Althorp collection, she went on with the renovation of the house and grounds. Gilded trim and red velvet spread through the public rooms of Althorp House like a blight, while frilly bright pink was the theme in the private rooms. "How can that woman spend so much money on such bad taste?" wondered Jane.

Every time Diana visited Althorp, she missed Grandmother Cynthia more. It seemed so wrong that the gentle, gracious Lady Spencer of Diana's childhood had been replaced with Raine, the new Lady Spencer. For Diana, the final outrage was the day she found the portrait of Robert, first Lord Spencer, missing from the grand staircase. Instead of the ancestor ennobled by King James I, a full-length portrait of Raine as a young woman smiled down on the entrance hall. She was wearing *pink*.

In London, Diana was still looking for a job she could be proud of. She finally found one, teaching children at the prestigious Vacani Dance School. She worked there for three months.

Then, Diana joined a ski party in Switzerland. She hadn't known the group ahead of time, but she made friends quickly. When they weren't skiing, they had pillow fights and made fun of one another in songs. Somehow the others found out that a picture of Prince Charles had hung over Diana's bed in the dormitory at West Heath, and they teased her about her royal "boyfriend."

"Oh yes," Diana retorted, "I'm certainly going to marry the Prince of Wales." At the moment, as she knew from reading the tabloids, he was smitten with Amanda Trumbull.

In the middle of her skiing holiday, Diana fell and tore the tendons in her left ankle. She had to give up her job at the dance school. Back in London, she took odd jobs as housecleaner, including working for her sister Sarah. Sarah's apartment-mate was embarrassed to have Diana scrubbing their toilet and vacuuming the rugs, but Diana rather liked the work. Anyway, she was glad to be doing something to please Sarah. Even knowing Ginge's problems, Diana admired her enormously.

CHAPTER 9

THE MOST ELIGIBLE BACHELOR IN THE WORLD

Diana was determined to make her own home in London—at least, until she met the man she would fall madly in love with and marry. In July 1979, she turned eighteen and now she could have part of her inheritance money. Also, her parents finally agreed she was old enough to have her own apartment, and they bought one for her. Sarah, who was working for a London real estate agency, found Diana a nice three-bedroom apartment on Coleherne Court, in the Sloane Square section of London. Diana rented the two extra rooms to friends from school.

Diana had never had so much fun. Living on her own, with friends, was like everything she'd enjoyed most about boarding school—

without those annoying classes. In fact, one of her roommates was her best friend from West Heath, Carolyn Pride.

Diana and her friends didn't drink, smoke, or use drugs. They took turns cleaning the apartment, Diana dancing around with yellow rubber gloves on her hands. The roommates didn't bother to cook most of the time. "Chocolate's a major food group, isn't it?" giggled Diana as she passed around a bag of candy.

Sloane Square was full of people like Diana and her roommates, young women from well-to-do English families. Known as "Sloane Rangers," they dressed in plaid skirts and sweaters as if they were still in the country, spoke in an upper-class boarding-school accent, and didn't take life too seriously. They socialized with young men from the same background.

Diana knew several young men, and they often came to the apartment or took her out to movies and the ballet. She even washed and ironed one boyfriend's shirts. But she wasn't serious about any of them, even James Gilbey of the London gin family. These men were only pals to have fun with and play pranks on. One night Diana and Carolyn mixed up a plaster of eggs and flour, took it to where James Gilbey's Alfa Romeo was parked, and smeared the sports car all over. "That'll pay him back for standing me up last night," said Diana.

Toward the end of August 1979, a shocking story burst into the news. Lord Louis Mountbatten, on vacation in Ireland, had been murdered. Irish terrorists had blown up his fishing boat.

"Poor Charles!" exclaimed Diana to her mother as they watched the state funeral for Lord Mountbatten on television. Lord Mountbatten had been Prince Charles's great-uncle, but he had been more like a father to him. Although the Prince of Wales had had years of training in controlling his feelings, his grief that day was plain to see. There was pain on his face and in every line of his body.

Diana's own eyes welled with sympathetic tears.

In September 1979, Diana started work at a new job. This one seemed ideal for her. She was hired by Young England Kindergarten to work with the littlest children three days a week. Diana's duties included preparing art projects for the children, taking them into the yard for playtime, and cleaning up after them. She loved her new job, and the children adored her.

Diana also babysat for an American couple with one little boy, Patrick. The mother, Mary Robertson, had no idea her babysitter was *Lady* Diana, but she was impressed at the way Diana and her baby bonded. Clearly there was nothing Diana would rather do than play blocks on the floor or take Patrick out in his stroller.

On weekends Diana often went to house parties in the country. In July 1980, her friend Philip de Pass invited her to Petworth, the estate of friends of his. The main event of the weekend was a polo match in which the Prince of Wales played with his team. Afterward the party returned to Petworth for a barbecue, and Diana sat down next to Charles on a bale of hay.

Diana knew that Charles had recently broken up with Anna Wallace, daughter of a wealthy Scottish landowner. But she wasn't thinking of that. In Diana's mind, Prince Charles was still the grieving great-nephew she'd seen at Lord Mountbatten's funeral last year.

Most people would have been afraid to mention such a painful event, but for Diana, it felt natural to give Charles her sympathy. "You looked so sad when you walked up the aisle at the funeral," she said simply. "It was the most tragic thing I've ever seen."

Charles looked startled for an instant, and Diana wondered if she had been too personal. Then he said in a husky voice, "Yes. It was—tragic." He picked up her hand and held it in both of his.

"My heart bled for you when I watched it,"

Diana went on. "I thought, *It's wrong, you are lonely, you should be with somebody to look after you.*"

"Ah, Diana . . ."

Diana wasn't sure whether Charles moved first to hug her, or she moved toward him first. But it seemed like the most natural thing in the world. This was just the way she would put her arms around any of her Sloane Square friends, or the little children at the kindergarten, when they needed a hug.

Prince Charles and Diana spent the rest of the evening together, talking and laughing. When Diana returned to London, she had a lot to report to her friend Carolyn.

"He must be smitten!" Carolyn squealed. "The most eligible bachelor in the world is smitten with our Duchess!"

"Don't be silly," said Diana. "What would the Prince of Wales want with a slightly pudgy young kindergarten teacher?" Diana didn't know that Lord Mountbatten, advising his great-nephew about marriage, had described a girl exactly like her. "A suitable, attractive and sweet-charactered girl," as he had put it.

Charles's future queen, Mountbatten had told him, should be about ten years younger than he was. She should be someone who had never been in love before. Her background must be aristocratic. She should be acquainted with the royal family so that she would understand the duties and responsibilities of a princess and queen.

Shortly after that weekend, Charles called Diana's apartment. Would she like to come to a concert with him that night and then have supper at Buckingham Palace? Diana's grandmother Ruth was in London, and she could accompany them as Diana's chaperone.

Diana was flattered and flustered. Charles really liked her! What would her sister Sarah say?

After the concert date, Charles invited Diana to a party on the royal yacht, *Britannia*. It was the week of the traditional regatta at Cowes. The *Britannia* was swarming with the prince's older, sophisticated friends, and Diana felt shy. "They were all over me like a bad rash," she told Carolyn afterward. "They were *inspecting* me."

The next month, Charles invited Diana to Balmoral Castle, the royal family's estate in the Scottish Highlands, for the Braemar Games. Queen Elizabeth was patron of the traditional Highland festivities, as Queen Victoria had been, and the royal family always attended. Diana's sister Jane Fellowes, who had just had a baby, would be there, since her husband was a member of the royal court. Diana could stay with Jane in the Fellowes' cottage.

During the days Charles and Diana fished in the Dee River and took walks in the hills. Every evening Charles and his guests dined with the queen. Prince Charles stayed with his grandmother the Queen Mother at Birkhall, her house on the grounds of Balmoral. Charles and his grandmother were very fond of each other, and Diana wondered if they talked about her at all. On one long walk over the heather-covered moors, Charles casually remarked to Diana that his grandmother thought he needed a good wife.

It was during this week that Diana was discovered by the media. Paparazzi, photographers who take candid shots of celebrities for a living, stalked Prince Charles as usual. One day when Diana and Charles went fishing, the paparazzi realized the prince was with a girl. If only they could snap a picture of the heir to the throne of England with a new girlfriend! Readers of the tabloids would be very interested to see such a picture, and so the tabloids would pay the paparazzi a good chunk of money for it.

Realizing what the photographers were up to, Diana hid behind the trees, and they didn't get a picture of her that day. But later they found out her name. On September 8, 1980, Diana's private life ended. A headline on the front page of the *Sun* shouted, HE'S IN LOVE AGAIN! LADY DI IS THE NEW GIRL FOR CHARLES. To go with the story, they'd dug up a picture of Diana at the polo match in July.

The next day at Young England Kindergarten, paparazzi showed up at the door. "Why don't you just give them what they want," Diana's boss suggested, "and maybe they'll leave you alone after that." Diana felt shy, but she took two of the children outside with her and posed.

Far from leaving Diana alone, the press went into a feeding frenzy. In the days and weeks afterward, the kindergarten could hardly function, with television crews around the building and paparazzi perching in nearby trees. The media found out where Diana lived and they haunted Coleherne Court, hoping for interviews and pictures. The phone rang all the time, from very early in the morning until very late at night, with reporters trying to get an exclusive story about the latest candidate for Princess of Wales.

In October, Diana went back to Balmoral in Scotland, this time as the guest of the Queen Mother. Prince Charles's grandmother was clearly happy that the prince was seriously interested in Lady Diana Spencer. For one thing, Diana was the granddaughter of the Queen Mother's best friend, Ruth Fermoy. For another thing, Charles seemed happy with Diana, and Diana seemed to be in love with him. While Charles was gone for the day on stag hunts, Diana sat with her grandmother and Charles's grandmother and worked on her needlepoint. The older women smiled approvingly at her.

But Diana wasn't entirely happy with her life as Prince Charles's new girlfriend. On the weekends, when she stayed with his friends or family, she was protected from the public. But in London, she was on her own. She began to understand how a fox running from a pack of hounds must feel. Paparazzi and reporters lurked around every corner; they breathed down her neck. Anytime she picked up a newspaper, she might see her own picture (usually head down, trying to avoid the camera). Driving over a bridge in London one day, she looked out to see an enormous billboard with a tabloid's headline: DI—THE REAL STORY!

Diana burst into tears. "I can't take this anymore," she sobbed. It was unbearable to have her privacy gone. And not only that—they were calling her "Di," a nickname she hated.

If Diana were engaged to Charles, she would be protected by Buckingham Palace. And that brought up another sore point: Why didn't Charles ask her to marry him? Did he really love her? Diana was tormented by doubts. She was sure she was in love with him—how did *he* feel?

In October, Charles took her to see Highgrove, the house in Gloucestershire he'd bought for himself. He loved the towering cedar tree in front and the walled garden, for which he had big plans. To Diana's surprise, he asked her to take charge of decorating the inside of the house. That didn't seem proper—unless he wanted her to live there with him.

In November, Charles left on an official visit to India and Nepal. Diana felt abandoned. He came back to England for Christmas, but he went to Windsor Castle with the rest of the royal family while Diana went to Althorp. Then Diana joined Charles at Sandringham for New Year, but still, he didn't propose.

Hordes of reporters and paparazzi staked out Sandringham, waiting for the answer to the Big Question: Is Diana The One? The royal family, although they were used to being followed by the media, lost their tempers. Charles told reporters he wished the editors of their newspapers a particularly nasty New Year. Even the queen snapped at them: "Why don't you all go away?"

Diana couldn't stand the tension anymore. She decided on a ploy that always seemed to work in Barbara Cartland's romance novels. She planned a trip to Australia in February, to visit her mother and stepfather on their sheep ranch. Maybe Charles would miss her the way she'd missed him when he went to India.

But at the beginning of 1981, before Diana could leave for Australia, Charles left on a skiing trip in Switzerland. There, he must have come to a decision, because he called Diana from his friends' chalet. He wanted her to know that he had something important to ask her when he came back.

Diana went around in an excited daze. There was only one "important question" that Charles could ask her. She knew what it was. On February 6, she went to meet Charles at Windsor Castle.

CHAPTER 10
THE FAIRY-TALE WEDDING

Prince Charles's proposal was not very romantic. It didn't come out in a candlelit alcove, but rather as he was showing her the nursery at Windsor Castle. He didn't go down on one knee. Unlike the hero of the romance novel *Princess in Distress*, he didn't murmur, "This is real love, my darling, and its enchantment will remain with us for all time."

"I've missed you so much," said Charles. Pausing, he put his arm around her. "Will you marry me?"

Diana giggled nervously, not sure if he was joking. But Charles looked into her eyes, dead serious. "You need to understand, you wouldn't only be marrying me—you'd be marrying a way of life. A hard way of life. You'd be queen some day." He almost seemed to be apologizing to her. "Take some time to think it over."

"Of course I'll marry you!" Diana hardly heard what he was saying—except that at last he was asking her to become his princess. "Oh Charles, I love you so much! I love you, I love you!" She couldn't stop talking.

When Diana returned to the apartment on Coleherne Court, her friends rushed into her bedroom after her. "Well? Well?"

Smiling slowly, Diana savored the suspense. "Guess . . . what?" She fell backward onto her bed.

They jumped up and down, screaming, "He asked you!"

Diana grinned up at the other girls. "He did."

"What did you say?" they chorused.

"I said, 'Yes, please.'"

Carolyn whooped, "We have to celebrate!"

"No, we can't," said Diana, suddenly serious. "We have to keep this a secret until the palace announces our engagement. Oh—I'm going to burst!" She bounced up from her bed.

"Come on, let's get in my car. I'll drive you around my new home-to-be!"

Piling into Diana's little red Mini Metro, Diana and her friends drove around and around Buckingham Palace. It was very late at night, so not many people noticed the car full of girls or heard what they were shouting: "Here comes Princess Diana! Here comes *Queen* Diana! Long live the queen!"

Buckingham Palace officially announced the engagement on February 24. The night before, Diana hugged her friends at Coleherne Court good-bye. She was bubbling with excitement as she left for the palace with an armed Scotland Yard bodyguard. The bodyguard looked at her kindly. "This is the last night of freedom in your life," he said, "so make the most of it."

For just a moment, Diana froze. Surely royal life couldn't be as bad as all that? And besides, she told herself, love could overcome anything.

The day of the official announcement, Diana and Charles were interviewed on BBC TV.

Diana wore a bright blue suit and a blue-and-white-print blouse with a bow at the neck, as well as her engagement ring. The ring was set with a large oval sapphire, circled with brilliant-cut diamonds.

The BBC interviewer wanted to know how the couple felt. "I'm positively delighted and frankly amazed that Diana is prepared to take me on," said Charles.

"And in love?" asked the interviewer.

What a silly question! thought Diana. She giggled and rolled her eyes. "Of course."

"Whatever 'love' means," Charles added with a faint smile.

Diana felt a pang. Surely Charles loved her—why couldn't he just *say* it straight out? Well, Charles was like that. He'd been brought up to hide his feelings. He couldn't announce, as Lord Arkley had in *Princess in Distress*, "I did not know it was possible to be so happy and so very much in love!"

The wedding date was set for July 29. That gave them five months, which was not much time to prepare for "the Wedding of the Century," as the media were calling it. Frances Shand Kydd came from Scotland to help Diana plan.

As a soon-to-be princess, Diana needed a whole new wardrobe—a large one. With so many public appearances expected of her, Diana might have to change outfits several times a day, and look perfect every time. She needed a hairdresser and a makeup consultant.

To Diana's surprise, Queen Elizabeth didn't try to help her future daughter-in-law adjust to royal life. Their quarters at the palace were a mile apart, and Diana hardly ever saw the queen, except by appointment. The courtiers assigned to look after Diana gave her advice about royal etiquette and customs, but no one made her feel at home.

For Diana's first public appearance after the engagement, a charity gala, she chose a strapless black taffeta evening gown. It was the most sophisticated dress Diana had ever worn, and she thought she looked stunning. But when

Charles caught sight of her, he was stunned in a different way. "Are you out of your mind? You can't wear that. Black is for mourning."

Diana was hurt, then angry. "Well, it's the only suitable dress I have." They went out to face the paparazzi, who aimed their cameras at Diana's cleavage. She began to realize that her gorgeous new gown really was not suitable for a young woman engaged to the Prince of Wales. She was embarrassing her fiancé.

During the evening Diana tried to hold her head high, but she felt crushed. The only bright moment came when another guest took her by the arm. It was Princess Grace of Monaco, a woman Diana had always admired. "Wouldn't you like some time out?" the older woman whispered. "Come with me."

In the ladies' restroom, Diana blurted out, "Oh, it's dreadful! How can I stand it? Everyone looking at me, criticizing every little thing I do!" Under Princess Grace's kind gaze, she began to cry. "I'm so lonely!"

Princess Grace smiled at the younger

woman in her serene, lovely way. "Watch your makeup, dear." She handed her a tissue. "Try to laugh about it. And don't worry about the future, because"—she chuckled—"it'll get a lot worse."

Her Royal Highness of Monaco was right. At the end of March, Charles flew off to Australia for an official tour. He would be gone for five weeks. Diana was alone in her little suite in Buckingham Palace, a huge cold building of six hundred rooms. She missed her Coleherne Court friends dreadfully. Queen Elizabeth and Prince Philip were pleasant enough, but they and almost everyone else in the palace were too busy to pay much attention to Diana.

One of the queen's ladies-in-waiting, Lady Susan Hussey, was assigned to teach Diana how to behave. Of course Diana had been brought up to have perfect manners, but that wasn't enough. "You don't want to seem so . . . *enthusiastic*, my dear," explained Lady Susan. "For instance, in driving past a crowd, try not to wave more than once or twice. Notice how Her Majesty does it—just a calm lift of the hand." She smiled in what was meant to be a kind way. "After all, you are a princess, not a film star."

Diana blushed and smiled weakly. How could she help getting excited when she went out in public? All those people, waving and cheering, so excited to see *her*. Diana felt they deserved a big wave back and her biggest smile.

Most of the time Diana was proud of the role she played in public. She wasn't intimidated, as most young women would have been, at being around the royal family. Some of the tabloid stories, noting that Diana had worked as a housecleaner, called her a Cinderella, but of course that was nonsense. Grandmother Cynthia's words echoed in Diana's head: "My dearest Diana, always remember that you are a Spencer." The Spencers had been English aristocrats for centuries before the Windsors even arrived in England from Germany.

But Diana longed to hear Charles praise

her. He was away from the palace much of the time. Even when he was home, he seemed to take it for granted that she would take on her new royal life without complaining. She wanted so much for him to say, "Good job! You'll make a terrific princess!"

As the wedding approached, Diana didn't eat, or else she gobbled down a lot of food and then she was sick. She got thinner and thinner. Each time her ivory silk wedding gown was fitted, the seamstress had to take it in some more.

When Charles was with her, holding her hand and smiling at her, Diana felt that she was the luckiest girl in the world. At other times, she was sure she was making a terrible mistake. She burst into sobs at the wedding rehearsal, and again at one of Charles's polo games.

Shortly before the wedding, Diana's sisters came to Buckingham Palace for a private lunch with her. Diana blurted out her doubts to Sarah and Jane. "Maybe. . . ," she said in a shaky voice, "maybe I should call the whole thing off."

Sarah looked shocked, then laughed as if Diana had made a joke. Jane laughed too. "Bad luck, Duch! Your face is on all the souvenir tea towels, so you're too late to chicken out now."

It did seem that nothing could stop "the Wedding of the Century," as NBC was calling it, from taking place on July 29 at St. Paul's Cathedral. Eleven carriages were prepared to carry the royal party from Buckingham Palace to the cathedral. A guard of 600,000 policemen and soldiers were assigned to provide security for the event. The wedding would be televised, and 750 million people around the world would be watching.

Diana practiced walking down the palace ballroom with yards and yards of tissue paper fastened to her head. Her wedding veil would feel like that, dragging on the ground behind her.

The night before the wedding, Charles sent Diana a note. "I'm so proud of you and when you come up I'll be there at the altar for you tomorrow. Just look 'em in the eye and knock 'em dead." As Diana read these words, her heart melted. Charles loved her, and she loved him. That was all that mattered. She would do her part and make him even prouder of her.

On the morning of her wedding day, Diana's attendants dressed her in the ivory silk taffeta gown with thousands of pearls and sequins sewn on the bodice. She was wearing on her underskirts the traditional "something old," a piece of lace that had belonged to her ancestress Georgiana. "Something new," a gold horseshoe studded with diamonds, given by her father, was sewn inside her skirt along with "something blue," a blue bow. "Something borrowed" was her mother's pearl-and-diamond earrings.

Diana climbed into the hundred-year-old Glass Coach, kept for royal weddings. Her father sat beside her for the ride to St. Paul's Cathedral. Johnny Spencer had never really recovered from his stroke, but he was so proud and happy to be giving his youngest daughter away to the Prince of Wales. He waved out the coach window to the cheering crowds as if he were the prince.

I will *get Daddy through the ceremony,* Diana told herself. It helped her nerves to concentrate on someone else. Although her train was crumpled by the time they reached St. Paul's, she remained calm. Her attendants smoothed out the twenty-five feet of ivory silk, and Diana climbed the steps.

All Diana's dancing experience made her strong and graceful as she slowly, slowly walked down the 650-foot aisle of the cathedral. Her father had to lean on her arm instead of the other way around, since he usually walked with a cane. At the end of the long aisle, Charles was waiting in his admiral's uniform. His jacket was trimmed with gold braid and decorated with medals, and a gold sword was at his side.

As Diana came closer to the altar she could see Charles's face more and more clearly through her veil. In the heavy cascading bouquet she carried were Earl Mountbatten roses, symbolic of his beloved great-uncle. Diana felt such love for Charles; she felt she was bringing him joy to heal the terrible wound of Mountbatten's death. She had never been so deeply happy in her life.

"You look wonderful," whispered Charles.

"Wonderful for you," Diana whispered back.

Dr. Robert Runcie, the Archbishop of Canterbury, performed the ceremony. "This is the stuff of which fairytales are made," he told the congregation, "the Prince and Princess on their wedding day."

On the newlyweds' way back to Buckingham Palace for the wedding breakfast, church bells rang joyously all over London. The crowds cheered the royal couple and threw flowers at their carriage. Charles squeezed Diana's hand, and she knew he was as deeply touched as she was. The whole nation—the whole world—was rejoicing with them.

Charles teased Diana about a mistake she'd made during the ceremony, calling him "Philip

Charles Arthur George" instead of "Charles Philip Arthur George."

"Well, it's your own fault for having four names!" she teased him back. Diana felt weary, but very happy. She was married to her prince at long last.

CHAPTER 11
HAPPILY EVER AFTER?

Diana and Charles's honeymoon started with a few days at Broadlands, Mountbatten's country estate in Hampshire. Then they boarded *Britannia*, the royal yacht, and cruised the Mediterranean Sea for three weeks. The cruise wasn't as romantic as Diana had expected, since they had to dine with the naval officers every night and get up early on Sundays for the church service.

Also, Diana was beginning to think something was wrong. Deep down, she was afraid that Charles must be disappointed in her. Why else would he spend so much time reading?

"I *like* to read," he protested. Charles's favorite author was the anthropologist Laurens van der Post. He read passages aloud to her, trying to get her interested.

At first Diana made an effort to listen, but these books only reminded her of the O-level exams she'd failed. How could Charles love this stuff so much? He must think she was thick as a plank. She wandered around the yacht, making friends with the sailors and eating ice cream.

At the end of the cruise Diana and Charles flew to Scotland, where they were to spend a month at Balmoral with the rest of the court. Here, too, it was very different from what Diana had expected. She was familiar with the traditions of how royals ought to act, and how other people ought to act with them. Still, it felt so uncomfortable when the guests at Balmoral treated her like a porcelain princess on a mantel. They bowed or curtsied when they met her in the halls. They wouldn't call her "Diana"—she was "Your Royal Highness" the first time, and then "ma'am" after that.

The worst thing was, it wasn't any different with the royals themselves. Diana had thought that once she was inside the royal family, she'd see a different side of the Windsors. In private, they'd be relaxed and friendly with one another, wouldn't they? They were not.

Elizabeth II was perfectly pleasant—in fact, Diana began to wish she would yell at someone once in a while. No one touched the queen, and she hardly ever touched anyone else. From the way Elizabeth cuddled her dogs, thought Diana, she seemed to be more fond of those Welsh corgis than of her own children.

Everyone, including other members of the royal family, had to bow or curtsy to the queen. At the cocktail hour, Charles even had to serve his mother (the queen) and grandmother (the Queen Mother) their drinks before he offered his wife one. It was a little gesture, but to Diana it said that she didn't come first with her husband.

Among themselves, the royal family never seemed to talk about anything interesting. If Diana brought up a personal subject at the dinner table, no one would respond to her remark.

After an instant of silence, someone else would cover over the awkwardness by talking about the weather, or the family dogs. Even Charles, instead of supporting his wife, acted as if this was perfectly normal.

Princess Margaret, the queen's sister, was a little more relaxed than the others. She was considered the black sheep of the British royal family—she'd been the first royal to divorce since Henry VIII in the sixteenth century. "Call me Margo," she'd told Diana the first time they met.

When Diana complained about the way the royal family pretended nothing was wrong, Margaret smiled. "Oh, yes; don't we do that well? We call it 'ostriching.'" According to legend, the ostrich reacted to danger by burying its head in the sand. Likewise, the royal family seemed to think that if they ignored unpleasant things, those things would go away.

Diana did understand that she was supposed to put on a happy face in public. A press conference was scheduled for the Prince and

Princess of Wales, and they posed for photographers on the banks of the River Dee. Charles wore a Highland kilt, and Diana a tartan skirt and jacket. Diana gave a radiant smile as Charles kissed her hand. "I can thoroughly recommend married life," she told the reporters.

But the next morning, as Charles got dressed to go fishing in the rain, Diana said, "Charles—I want to go back to London."

"We can't just leave Balmoral," Charles said in a patient tone. "The court is here. We're the Prince and Princess of Wales—it's our job to be here."

"Balmoral is wet and—boring," Diana burst out.

Checking his fishing vest pockets, Charles raised his eyebrows. "Last year, you said Balmoral was your favorite place on earth."

Diana hung her head, baffled and miserable. Yes, last year she'd been blissfully happy in the drizzle at Balmoral. She'd gone for long, damp walks with Charles. While he was off fishing, she'd sat around the castle doing needlework with the other women. When the men went out shooting, she'd cheerfully helped bring their lunch into the muddy fields.

But now that she and Charles were married, Diana had expected they would spend most of their time alone together. Charles would gaze into her eyes and whisper things like, "My darling, I will make you happy." Instead, they spent evenings with the rest of the royal family.

One evening at dinner, as dessert was being offered, Diana's eyes filled with tears. Queen Elizabeth, without exactly looking at Diana, seemed to send her a message from the head of the table: *Pull yourself together.* Diana slumped, afraid she was going to burst into sobs any minute. She looked around the table for help, but each person who met her eyes glanced quickly away.

Swallowing a sob, Diana made a gulping noise. Then Charles did look at her, but Diana could see he was only embarrassed. Diana pushed back her chair and murmured, "Please excuse me." She fled to their suite.

Diana thought that if Charles loved her, he would rush after her to comfort her. But she sobbed alone on her bed for half an hour before he showed up. Sitting down on the bed, Charles asked, "Diana, are you ill? One doesn't leave the dinner table before the queen."

Shocked, Diana raised her face from the pillow. Her eyes were red and swollen. "How can you talk to me that way?" she asked. "Don't you *care* how I feel?"

Charles heaved a sigh. "Of course I care," he said, "but you are a princess now. It's your duty to control your feelings."

"But it wasn't some kind of grand state dinner tonight!" exclaimed Diana. "It was a family dinner."

"That makes no difference," said Charles. "You can't just do whatever you like." He sighed again. "I tried to tell you this when I asked you to marry me."

Diana couldn't control her feelings, and she got worse and worse. Some days she sobbed for hours, and some days she kicked the furniture and shouted. She was still losing weight. There were hollows under the cheekbones of her once-plump face, and her skin was pale.

Finally Charles was seriously worried about Diana's health. He took her to London, where she saw several doctors and psychologists. They weren't much help—except that they found out Diana was pregnant.

Pregnant women sometimes go through very emotional times, so Charles and Diana, as well as the rest of the royal family, assumed this had been her problem all along. Diana was now also suffering from morning sickness, but she was happy to think there was a baby—her and Charles's baby—on the way.

At the end of October the Prince of Wales took his princess to visit his own principality, the part of the kingdom from which his title came. Wales had been a trouble spot for English royalty for hundreds of years. The Welsh had never lost their resentment over being conquered by England in 1282. During Charles's investiture in 1969, there had been anti-English demonstrations and even a bomb explosion. Now there were some protests along the royal couple's tour, and once a protester managed to get close enough to spray their car with an aerosol paint can.

But most of the Welsh people were ready to love their new princess, and Diana was ready to love them. Dressed in red and green, the national colors of Wales, she walked up to the crowds with a radiant smile. The queen's lady-in-waiting had instructed Diana how to approach a crowd along a walking route. Queen Elizabeth always wore long white gloves, and once in a while she would shake someone's hand. Diana, gloveless, leaned into the crowd to hug children and touch everyone she could reach. It was so obvious to her—they wanted to be touched, and she wanted to touch them.

All during the trip Diana felt nauseated and weary from her pregnancy. "I can't do this, I just can't," she sobbed before every appearance. But each time she got out of the car and saw the people's eager faces, she felt a surge of strength. At the final stop, Caernarvon Castle, it poured rain, but the royal couple walked the planned route, anyway.

Diana kept leaving the umbrella held for her by her lady-in-waiting, Anne Beckwith-Smith. Rain or no rain, she *had* to stoop down, hug children, and take the bunches of flowers they held out. "Di, Di!" people called. "Over here, over here!" The plume on Diana's beige designer hat drooped wetly, her beige designer coat was sodden, and her shoes squished as she walked.

Charles, walking on the other side of the street, didn't get nearly as much attention. He joked to the crowd, "Well, at least I know my place now—I'm a carrier of flowers for my wife."

Through her happiness, Diana became aware that the people on her side of the street felt lucky, and the people on Charles's side were disappointed. She whispered to her lady-in-waiting, "It's a bit embarrassing, what can we do about it? They keep moving to my side."

Later she saw the headline in a Welsh newspaper: DIANA: THE QUEEN OF HEARTS.

On June 21, 1982, Diana made headlines in a different way. Her first child, William Arthur Philip Louis, was born in London. Diana and Charles posed outside St. Mary's Hospital. They took turns holding their son, a little bundle in a white crocheted blanket, for the cameras.

Diana knew she looked dowdy in her green polka-dot maternity dress, but today she didn't care. The long, miserable pregnancy—nine months of feeling sick and exhausted—was over. She'd done what was expected of her: produce an heir to the throne of England, next in line to become king after Charles. More important, she had her own dear little baby to feed and change and bathe.

Charles assumed that his children would be brought up by an old-fashioned nanny who ruled the nursery, as he and his sister and brothers had been. In fact, he wanted to hire

Mabel Anderson, the same nanny who'd supervised the royal tea party at Sandringham when Diana was six. But Diana was determined that William's nanny would be only her assistant, not a mother substitute. She hired Barbara Barnes, a younger, less experienced nanny.

Charles doted on William just as much as Diana did, and he was happy to take his turn bathing the baby and changing his diapers. He read dozens of books on baby and child care and became something of an expert. "Charles knows so much about babies, he can have the next one," joked Diana.

But Diana was delighted to see her husband with their son, and she often described their latest high jinks to the people she met. When William was a little older and started fussing about taking his bath, Charles tried to encourage "Willie Wombat," as he called his son, by getting in the bathtub with him. "There was soap and water everywhere," said Diana with a giggle.

In September 1982, the royal court, including Charles, Diana, and little William, went to Balmoral as usual. While they were there, Princess Grace of Monaco died suddenly in a car crash. Someone would have to represent the British royal family at her funeral, and Diana immediately volunteered to go.

The funeral was a sad event, but Diana was glad to pay tribute to the woman she'd felt a special connection with. Princess Grace had been so understanding with her on that uncomfortable evening when Diana had worn the wrong dress. And Diana was proud that, for this event, she represented England with dignity.

The next spring, Charles and Diana traveled to Australia on an official visit. It wasn't usual for a royal couple to bring little children on such a trip, but Diana insisted on bringing Prince William. She felt she couldn't stand to be away from him for the six-week tour. So William and his nanny were settled at a sheep ranch, where Diana and Charles could visit him in between official engagements. William crawled for the first time during the trip.

As it turned out, the interludes with their son were also a chance for the prince and princess to escape for some private time together. Away from the crowds and the photographer, they enjoyed each other's company.

Outside England and working with her husband, Diana felt close to him. Charles seemed so pleased with her. At every public appearance in Australia and New Zealand, thousands of people turned out to see the new princess. Again, they all wanted Diana, not Charles, to walk on their side of the street. Charles joked about it, though. He was tender and attentive with Diana, and she glowed.

Still, all the attention from the crowds was frightening to Diana at times. It was like being a rock star, except that rock stars actually wanted all the publicity they could get. Sometimes Diana loved being treated like a goddess. Sometimes she wanted to scream, "It's just me, Diana—an ordinary person!"

CHAPTER 12

THE PEOPLE'S PRINCESS

At the beginning of 1984, Diana became pregnant again. In spite of feeling nauseated and tired much of the time, she had a good year in some ways. Charles traveled on official visits a great deal, but at home he was especially sweet to her. Even the queen praised her daughter-in-law publicly. That April a spokesman for Buckingham Palace announced, "The Queen is very proud of the Princess's activities around the world and at home."

On September 15, Diana and Charles's second child, Henry Charles Albert David (they called him Harry), was born. Diana had thought carefully about how to introduce two-year-old William to his baby brother. Now she made a point of greeting him outside her hospital room. Picking him up, she hugged him close as she took him to see little Harry for the first time.

Diana knew from tests that the baby was a boy. But she hadn't told Charles, since she knew he'd wanted a girl. "Oh, it's a boy," he said at his first glimpse of the new baby. "And he's even got rusty hair."

Charles's remarks were only his way of joking, but Diana was hurt. Obviously the red hair came from her side of the family. And how *could* he talk like that about their darling new baby?

Meanwhile, Diana the self-conscious teenager, dressing in ordinary skirts and sweaters, had become Princess Diana, a world leader in fashion. She discovered that she looked stunning in fashionable clothes, and she had the dancer's poise to carry them off. Designers, of course, were eager to see the Princess of Wales in their creations.

Most of the Windsors were the opposite of stylish—some called the queen downright dowdy. Princess Margaret had been one of the few in the royal family with a flair for fashion, but she was much older than Diana. Now the British were excited to have a glamorous princess again.

Diana, Princess of Wales, had become a celebrity in the way that rock stars and movie stars are celebrities. The rest of the royal family was not comfortable with this. The Windsor way, of which Queen Elizabeth was the foremost example, was quiet dignity. The royal family could have endearing little quirks, like the queen's pack of Welsh corgis or the Queen Mother's flowery hats. But appearing regularly on the front pages of the tabloids was Not Done.

Also, Diana had a knack for grabbing media attention away from the other royals. In November 1984, Diana attended the opening of Parliament. This state occasion was televised, and the focus was supposed to be on the queen's speech. Diana was only a member of the audience, but she looked especially striking with her hair in a new short style. All the cameras turned away from the queen and toward Diana.

One of Diana's best friends these days was Sarah Ferguson, another "Sloane Ranger." Gossiping and giggling with "Fergie" connected Diana with the carefree days before her marriage, and she made a point of having lunch with her once a week. Redheaded Fergie was spirited and funny, and Diana felt she could trust her not to repeat what she said.

As William and Harry grew, the Waleses settled into their two new homes. When they were in London, they lived in Kensington Palace. Jane and her husband, Robert Fellowes, had a house on the palace grounds, and Diana often took her children to play with Jane's.

The Waleses' country home, Highgrove, was a nine-bedroom Georgian house on 350 acres, about 100 miles west of London. Diana liked her mother's taste in interior design, and she hired the same designer to work with her on Highgrove. Charles spent long hours in the gardens, creating beautiful scenes such as the meadow of red poppies and yellow corn marigolds along the drive to the house. Near the house he restored a brick-walled fruit and vegetable garden with a pond and fountain in the center.

In June 1985, Diana had Sarah Ferguson invited to Royal Ascot week at Windsor Castle. Charles's younger brother Prince Andrew, now in his mid-twenties, was immediately attracted to bouncy, cheerful Fergie. Charles liked her, too, because Fergie was always in a good mood. "Why can't you be more like Fergie?" he asked Diana.

Diana was hurt. In fact, she *had* been all bubbly and good-humored—before their wedding. She could still be like that, in fact, only not with Charles.

In September 1985, William started nursery school. This was a big event because Charles and his sister Anne, like their parents and grandparents, had been taught at home by a governess. So had Diana and her sisters, until their mother left home. But Diana was deter-mined that her sons would have a more normal upbringing. So off William went to Mrs. Mynors's kindergarten in Notting Hill, accompanied by his bodyguard and watched by 150 photographers.

Meanwhile, an unflattering article about the Prince and Princess of Wales appeared in *Vanity Fair*, an American magazine. The article claimed that Diana was "obsessed with her image," Charles was a wimp, and the Waleses' marriage was in trouble. In October the Prince and Princess of Wales fought back by appearing in a television interview.

Diana was sick with nervousness before the TV appearance, and she practiced hard to prepare for it. But the interview succeeded brilliantly as publicity. Afterward, the *Daily Mirror* called Diana and Charles "a smashing royal couple," and the *Sun* gushed, "Di and Charles are so very much in love."

Later that fall the Prince and Princess of Wales visited the United States. They were on the cover of *Time* magazine, and their opening of an exhibit on British country homes was the event of the Washington social season. President Reagan gave a White House ball in their honor, and Diana danced with movie stars as well as the president. The *Daily Mirror* ran a story about the ball with the headline: DISCO QUEEN DIANA UPSTAGES JOHN TRAVOLTA.

Prince Charles could see that glamorous Princess Diana was upstaging not only him, but the whole purpose of the visit: the British exhibition at the National Gallery in Washington, D.C. In his speech at the opening of the exhibit, he tried to make a joke of it. He explained deadpan why such enormous crowds had flocked to see the royal couple: "They have all turned out to see my new clothes."

Charles's clothes were always well-tailored but boringly conventional. Diana, in contrast, wore a different and stunning outfit every day. For the opening of the exhibit in Washington she wore a pearl and diamond tiara (a Windsor family heirloom), and a cream-colored evening dress with a hip-length lace bodice and a taffeta skirt.

Even when Diana was trying to please Charles, she seemed to do the wrong thing. For instance, back in London she arranged to do a dance number onstage at the Royal Opera House during a royal gala. The dance was a surprise birthday present for Charles, and she had rehearsed her routine to a pop song for weeks. At last, Diana felt, she was expressing her true self, the joy she took in dancing.

After Diana's dance, the audience applauded as if they would never stop. But Charles was embarrassed. Dancing in public like that, he told her later, was behavior unbefitting a future queen. Besides, her silver silk costume had revealed how frighteningly thin she had gotten.

Diana was not well. Ever since before her wedding she had suffered off and on from bulima, an eating disorder. She had been treated by several different doctors and psychotherapists, but none of them seemed to help. The basic problem was that she was unhappy with her marriage and her way of life. As Diana confided to Fergie, she wanted out. Fergie introduced her to an astrologer, Penny Thornton, and Diana had her chart read. The astrologer talked Diana out of leaving Charles.

The trouble was, Diana and Charles had almost nothing in common. He hated London and loved the country. His favorite activities were gardening, horseback riding, and reading. He liked to spend time by himself or with a few like-minded people; one of the guests he regularly invited to Highgrove was the anthropologist Sir Laurens van der Post.

Diana, on the other hand, thrived on the excitement and glamour of city life. She loved shopping, dancing, watching TV, and talking with any friendly person who happened to be around—even the servants. Unlike Charles, she would often wander into the kitchen at Highgrove to munch on chocolate or eat a cup of yogurt and chat. She made friends with the servants, remembering their birthdays with presents.

Diana became especially good friends with the Highgrove butler, Paul Burrell, and with her personal protection officer, Barry Mannakee. She would ask Mannakee's advice about clothes and model new dresses for him. When she was unhappy, she felt free to cry and tell him her troubles. Unlike Charles, Mannakee would always listen sympathetically and give her a hug.

It had gotten to the point where Diana and Charles could be happy together only when they were with their children. They were both devoted parents, in spite of the fact that they had a nanny and other servants to look after William and Harry. Charles would rush home from his official duties to play Big Bad Wolf with the boys.

One of Diana's special activities with William and Harry was to take them shopping at Harrods. The department store would close to the public that day so that Diana and her boys could shop undisturbed. She ran around the store squealing with the boys, but she encouraged them to pick out toys for other children as well as themselves.

By the end of February 1986, Prince Andrew and Fergie were engaged. Diana was delighted. Soon Fergie would be the Duchess of York, and Diana would have a girlfriend in the royal family.

Fergie egged Diana on to act as silly and immature as she wanted, taking her back to her happy times at school. In July 1986, the night before Fergie's wedding to Prince Andrew, the two women dressed up as policewomen and tried to stop Andrew's car from entering Buckingham Palace. The following winter, on a ski vacation at Klosters in Switzerland, they clowned around on the slopes in front of photographers, pushing each other like little children. Charles seemed to think the Duchess of York was acting a little *too* bubbly in public, and he frowned at them. But they couldn't stop laughing. At the chalet that night, they had a pillow fight. And the next summer at Royal Ascot, dressed to the nines, they giggled and poked a courtier walking ahead of them with their parasols.

It was good that Diana had a new friend in the royal family, because she had just lost another friend. Her protection officer, Barry Mannakee, had been transferred to other duties away from the princess. In July 1987, she heard that he had been killed in an accident on a motorbike. Diana was frantic with grief. She even imagined that some of the royal staff who disapproved of her had had him murdered.

One reason for Diana's distrust of the people around her was that they really were deceiving her in some ways. The worst thing was that Charles was spending time with an old girl-friend, Camilla Parker Bowles. Charles insisted that he and Camilla were only good friends now, but Diana didn't believe him. She was convinced that Camilla was, and always had been, the woman he truly loved.

In spite of Diana's unhappiness with her life in the royal family, she still had fits of trying to do what they expected of her. Since the Windsors were all devoted to horses and riding, she decided to overcome her childhood fear. She asked James Hewitt, an army officer who sometimes played polo against Charles, to give her riding lessons. They practiced in Hyde Park, where the royal family usually rode when they were in London. Diana began to confide in Hewitt, telling him how unhappy she was in her marriage, even telling him about her struggles with an eating disorder.

Before long she was deeply involved in a relationship with tall, handsome, devoted James Hewitt. Their affair was like a Barbara Cartland romance, especially the story of Mariska, a princess married to a man who makes her life miserable. Lord Arkley falls passionately in love with Mariska and finally saves her life. The title of that story was *Princess in Distress*.

CHAPTER 13

THE WAR OF THE WALESES

In January 1987, five-year-old William started classes at Wetherby, a full-time school. Diana was proud of his manners—most of the time. At a children's tea party, he lost his temper and threw his food on the floor. The nanny in charge tried to make him clean up the mess. "When I'm King I'm going to send my knights round to kill you!" he shouted.

Diana loved being William and Harry's mother, but she wasn't happy with her role as Princess of Wales. So far, she'd done nothing but appear in one designer outfit after another. That was very glamorous, but what did it really matter? She longed for a chance to do something that would make a difference.

In April 1987, the first hospital ward in

England for AIDS (autoimmune deficiency syndrome) was due to be opened. People were frightened of AIDS, a deadly new disease, and not much was understood about it. Many people believed that you could catch AIDS just by touching someone with the disease, or even by being in the same room. Michael Adler, the doctor in charge of the clinic, asked if a member of the royal family would appear at the opening. He thought it would reassure the public to see one of the royals in the AIDS clinic.

Princess Diana agreed to appear. More than that, she did not wear gloves, and she shook hands with the AIDS patients. This was the best possible publicity for the new AIDS ward and for changing the public attitude toward AIDS. Pictures of Diana, with her warm, natural smile, touching people with AIDS, appeared in newspapers and TV broadcasts all over the world.

As for Diana, the AIDS visit awoke a talent in her that had been unused since her West

Heath days. Sitting by the bedside of someone who was desperately sick, holding hands, she felt peaceful in a deep, quiet way. She gladly offered to help with the National AIDS Trust, and she visited clinics in Scotland. She was happy she could use her celebrity for a good cause.

Meanwhile, Diana and Charles's marriage went steadily downhill. What made it even more painful was that the whole world knew they weren't getting along. Gossip about their marriage was repeated not only in the tabloids, but in respectable publications like the *London Times* and *Time* magazine.

The Prince and Princess of Wales, the media reported, were leading separate lives. Diana lived at Kensington Palace, and Charles lived at Highgrove. Some weekends Diana came to Highgrove with the children, but then usually Charles would arrange to be somewhere else. The royal couple did manage to be polite to each other at events for their children, such as Sports Day at William's school in 1987.

(Diana won the mother's 200-yard race.) The Prince and Princess of Wales also came to watch three-year-old Harry playing the part of a goblin (he stuck his tongue out at the photographers) in his Christmas play.

After several painful discussions, Diana and Charles agreed to lead separate private lives but appear together on official occasions. In January 1988, they traveled to Australia, representing the queen at the Australian national bicentennial celebration. But it was clear that the public and the media were more interested in Diana than in Charles, and Diana couldn't resist showing off her power.

At the grammar school in Melbourne that Charles had once attended, a photo opportunity was set up. Charles's old music teacher hauled out a cello and urged Charles to play. Charles hadn't touched a cello in years, but he started sawing away like a good sport. Then Diana deliberately walked in front of the cameras to the piano, sat down at the keyboard, and began playing a Rachmaninoff piece. She still played fairly well, and her performance made Charles look foolish.

By now the Prince and Princess of Wales had a hard time being polite to each other in public, let alone pretending to be happy together. Both of them did things to punish each other. Diana would think of excuses to keep William and Harry from going to watch their father play polo, even though the boys enjoyed those outings. Besides watching their father play, they liked to feed lumps of sugar to the ponies or crawl into the ambulance car to play doctors.

Charles was good at making cutting remarks, as when he found a headline and read it to her: "'Difficult Di Causes Malice at the Palace'—sounds about right to me." On one of the rare occasions when he and Diana had dinner together, he made a heartless reference to her eating disorder. As the butler set her plate in front of her, he wondered aloud, "Is that going to reappear later? Seems rather a waste."

With her own marriage in trouble, Diana

was distressed to hear in 1988 that her mother was getting divorced again. Not only that, but Frances talked to the press about her famous daughter, implying that her divorce was partly due to Diana's high-profile way of life. Didn't Frances understand how disloyal that was?

When Diana was younger, her grandmother Ruth had explained the Queen Mother's policy about family matters. In her view, the royal family and everyone connected with it should remain "utterly oyster" about their private lives. Like an oyster in its shell, they should stay clamped shut against all attempts to pry information out of them. The Queen Mother had a point, Diana realized now.

By 1990 Diana was seriously thinking of leaving Charles. The question was, how to do it without looking bad in the public's eyes? She heard that Andrew Morton, a journalist, was planning a biography of her. Maybe, she thought, she should give him inside information that would embarrass Charles and his family.

That August, Diana consulted a different

astrologer to help her make the decision. He told her he saw "scandal" and "long-term transformation" in her stars. He also commented that she was very angry. Of course anyone who knew Diana could see that she was angry.

In June 1990, Charles broke his arm playing polo. It didn't heal properly, and in September he went into the hospital for surgery to correct it. Diana dutifully visited Charles in the hospital, but clearly he didn't want her around. Leaving his suite, she visited other parts of the hospital, especially the intensive care ward. She comforted a man named Peter Hickling and his family as his wife was dying of a brain hemorrhage. She sat with a patient named Dean Woodward, in a coma because of a car accident.

Using the media in her war with Charles, Diana encouraged the idea that she was warm and loving with their children, while Charles was cold and distant. Diana knew that wasn't true, but she didn't mind seeing Charles suffer from it a bit. In April 1991, she took William and Harry to an amusement park. She and the boys were photographed having a high time together, Diana shrieking as loudly as they did on the rides.

The next day the headline in the *Daily Mail* read, CHARLES THE ABSENT FATHER: WHY THE PRINCE SHOULD SPEND MORE TIME WITH HIS SONS. This was not exactly fair. While Charles wouldn't take his sons to an amusement park, he did spend time with them in quieter ways. As he worked in the gardens at Highgrove, William and Harry followed their father around. He shared with them his fascination with the plants and animals and his love for natural beauty.

Diana and Charles both struggled to shield their sons from their marital problems, but it wasn't possible. The boys sometimes heard their parents' bitter arguments. After one screaming match between Diana and Charles at Highgrove, Diana ran into the bathroom, sobbing. A moment later she noticed a bunch of tissues being pushed under the bathroom door. "Mummy," said William's voice, "I hate to see you sad."

In June 1991, it was Prince William, now almost nine years old, who was in the hospital. A friend at school had accidentally hit him in the head with a golf club. Diana and Charles both rushed to the hospital, sick with worry. The doctors discovered a fracture in William's skull and they wanted to operate to relieve the pressure on his brain. They told the parents that the surgery wasn't tricky at all and that William would almost certainly be fine.

Charles decided, on the doctors' advice, to leave the hospital. His schedule for the evening called for him to act as host for foreign dignitaries, and he thought it was reasonable to be away from William that long. Diana took this as further evidence of her husband's hardheartedness. She was satisfied to see a headline on the next day's front page of the *Sun*, asking Charles, WHAT KIND OF A DAD ARE YOU?

In July 1991, Diana turned thirty. Charles offered to give her a birthday party, but Diana had no intention of spending her birthday with Charles's "stuffy old friends." Her idea of a happy birthday was attending a fund-raiser for a children's hospice. She was photographed at the hospice, blowing out her candles with a girl suffering from cystic fibrosis.

Although Diana often felt lonely and isolated, she found many friends to confide in. One of them was Adrian Ward-Jackson, a supporter of the Royal Ballet and the deputy chairman of the AIDS Crisis Trust. He was seriously ill with AIDS himself, and for months Diana had been visiting him and spending hours with him.

In August the royal court went on their annual retreat at Balmoral. While she was there in Scotland, Diana got the news that her friend was at the point of death. Although it was customary for a member of the court to ask the queen's permission to leave, Diana simply took off. Driving all night, she was in London the next day to be at Adrian's bedside.

The royal family wanted her to return

promptly to Scotland, but Diana insisted that her place was with her friend. At Balmoral, she had been doing nothing except gossiping and acting silly with Fergie. In Adrian's hospital room, she felt a deep sense of purpose and peace. She remained there until he died a few days later.

During that winter Diana made several visits to homeless shelters. One time she was accompanied by Cardinal Basil Hume, head of the Catholic Church in England and Wales. Many of the young people in the shelters were there because of drug or alcohol problems, too down-and-out to be polite to royalty. One young man, not recognizing the princess, called her "Gorgeous." The cardinal was horrified at such disrespect, but Diana only laughed. She felt more at ease with these people in desperate circumstances than she did with the courtiers at Buckingham Palace.

By 1992 the royal family was becoming increasingly unpopular in Britain. The country had been suffering through an economic depression for the last three years while the royal family was living in luxury at public expense. There was talk of doing away with the monarchy entirely. If Queen Elizabeth's family couldn't even behave in a dignified way, what was the point of having royalty?

In February the queen sent Diana and Charles to India on an official visit, trying to keep up appearances. Diana had hoped to meet Mother Teresa, the saintlike nun known for her work with the poor, on this trip. Mother Teresa happened to be in Rome, being treated for an illness, but Diana visited her Sisters of Mercy in Calcutta. She was photographed ladling out food for hungry people.

While Charles was busy with his official duties, Diana went by herself to see the Taj Mahal. The Taj Mahal is world-famous as one of the most romantic settings, a marble mausoleum built by a prince grieving over the death of his beloved wife. Diana was photographed looking sad as she sat on a bench in front of the Taj, the beautiful monument to married love. Charles had once promised to take Diana to the Taj Mahal, the tabloids reported, but now he was "too busy."

A few days later, Charles played in a polo match. This event gave Diana another opportunity to express her true feelings about her marriage. Diana was expected to present the prizes to the winning polo team, which happened to be Charles's team.

In years past Diana and Charles had often kissed affectionately after his polo matches, but those times were gone forever. This time, she turned her head away at the last minute. Charles was photographed looking silly as he kissed her neck. To add to the irony, it was the day before Valentine's Day.

After the India tour, Diana went alone to Rome to meet Mother Teresa. Diana deeply admired Mother Teresa, and she longed for her personal blessing. The little, bent-over nun told the tall, glamorous princess, "To heal other people you have to suffer yourself."

Diana's eyes filled with tears. "My life is torture," she said. They prayed together.

While Diana arranged photo-ops to embarrass Charles, she knew that much more damaging publicity for the Prince of Wales was on the way. She'd decided to cooperate with Andrew Morton in his biography of her, *Diana: Her True Story.* She'd given Carolyn Bartholomew and other close friends permission to talk frankly to Morton. She'd also talked to him herself at length over the phone. The book was due to appear in June.

Meanwhile, Diana's father, Johnny Spencer, had never fully recovered from his near-fatal illness in 1978. In March 1992, he died of a heart attack. Diana happened to be with Charles and their sons at a ski resort in Austria when she heard the news. She did not want her husband to escort her back to England or even attend the funeral, but he came, anyway. Although Charles didn't have Diana's knack for publicity, he knew it would have looked extremely hard-hearted if he had ignored his father-in-law's death.

In May, Charles sat beside Diana and the boys at a memorial service for Johnny Spencer in Westminster Abbey. The rest of the royal family sat with them in the front pew. Diana thought how proud her father would have been. Just a few years ago he'd said how proud he was of Diana, because she and the Pope were now the two most famous people in the world.

Tears came to Diana's eyes as she remembered how much Johnny Spencer had loved his grandsons William and Harry. He'd had a special tree house built for the boys at Althorp, and he'd let them ride their pedal cars down the elegant corridors of Althorp House. He used to chuckle over the time William showed him around the farm at Highgrove and made him climb over a gate. "I can't open it, Grandpa," said William firmly, "otherwise the animals will get out."

Diana's brother, Charlie, now Earl Spencer, hated his stepmother, Raine, as much as ever.

He made her leave Althorp immediately after the funeral and fired all her employees. He set about erasing all traces of her years at Althorp, down to the last little detail. He even removed Barbara Cartland's romance novels from the Althorp gift shop. Meanest of all, he arranged to have Raine sit apart from the rest of the Spencer family at the memorial service.

Diana had been just as angry as her brother and sisters at the way Raine had taken over Johnny Spencer and their ancestral home, Althorp. However, she felt Charlie was wrong to be so disrespectful to their father's widow. In the following years, she began to get together with Raine now and then for lunch in London. Diana had to admire Raine's spunk, and besides, she could be very amusing.

By this time rumors were going around royal circles that the Prince and Princess of Wales were on the point of separating. Charles and Diana had each hired lawyers, in case it came to that. But the final straw was the publication, in June 1992, of *Diana: Her True Story*. It was first serialized in the *Sunday Times,* then published in book form. When reporters asked Diana if she had contributed information to the book, she answered, "I have not cooperated with this book in any way." The queen and her advisers did not believe her. How else could Morton have discovered all the embarrassing details in the book?

The queen was right: It was Diana who'd told Andrew Morton that she suffered from an eating disorder, caused by her unhappy role in the royal family. She'd told him she suspected that Charles had been carrying on an inappropriate relationship with Camilla Parker Bowles since before their wedding. What was almost worse, she'd told him that Queen Elizabeth was not very helpful to her when she first moved into Buckingham Palace.

Diana: Her True Story was an immediate bestseller, and most of the millions of people who read it sided with Diana. Charles was horrified to see his marriage in print, sounding like a soap opera. This was a humiliating blow to the dignity of the royal family.

But Diana was comfortable with soap operas and their open displays of emotion. She knew that most British people watched soap operas on TV, and so did she. She would often chat about a popular soap opera to people on the street as a way of making a connection.

Of course Diana knew she'd broken the rule that members of the royal family had to remain "utterly oyster" about their private lives. Anyone who broke this rule risked being shut out, immediately and forever. Diana was fearful of what would happen to her, but at the same time she felt the royal family deserved to be exposed as unfeeling and petty. She'd worked for them all these years, she felt, without any appreciation or encouragement.

From this point on, Prince Charles and Princess Diana waged open war for public opinion. Other journalists released information they had kept secret until now out of respect for the royal family. One was a tape of Diana and her old friend James Gilbey flirting on the telephone. (He called her "Squidgy.") Another was a tape of Charles chatting intimately with his old girlfriend Camilla Parker Bowles.

Long before Charles thought of marrying Diana, he had been taught that, once he married, he could never divorce. After *Diana: The True Story* came out, he decided he wanted to end their marriage, anyway. Queen Elizabeth agreed to allow a legal separation, although she still would not allow a divorce. The queen felt that the Prince and Princess of Wales must stay married—technically, at least.

Diana agreed to the separation, too, but she had very mixed feelings. On the one hand, she wanted out of her miserable marriage. On the other hand, she remembered all too well how she had felt at the age of six when her own mother had left her father. How could she do that to William and Harry?

CHAPTER 14
DIANA'S GIFT

From Buckingham Palace the question was: How could Diana do this to the royal family? As far as Queen Elizabeth and her advisers were concerned, the year 1992 had been one public relations disaster after another. In April the Princess Royal, Charles's sister Anne, had divorced her husband, Captain Mark Phillips. In August, when the royal family were at Balmoral as usual, a tabloid printed an embarrassing picture of Fergie on vacation with John Bryan, her financial adviser. It was clear that Fergie and Prince Andrew, too, were headed for divorce.

To make things worse for the Windsors, in November, Windsor Castle caught fire and was badly damaged. Queen Elizabeth, in a scheduled public speech, said frankly that 1992 had been an *annus horribilis*—Latin for "horrible year."

In December 1992, Prime Minister John Major made an announcement to Parliament. The Prince and Princess of Wales, with the agreement of the queen, had decided to separate. Diana, listening to the prime minister on her car radio, felt a terrible sadness. The fairy-tale royal marriage had been over for some years, but this was the first official acknowledgment.

Diana's separation from Charles also caused a painful estrangement from some of her own family. Her grandmother Ruth Fermoy, loyal above all to the royal family, sympathized with Charles and criticized Diana. Diana's brother-in-law Sir Robert Fellowes, now the queen's private secretary, was devoted to the British monarchy, and when he discovered that Diana had lied about her cooperation with Andrew Morton's biography, he no longer trusted her. Jane, as his wife, was naturally loyal to her husband. As a result, Diana felt that she could no longer trust her sister.

Diana assumed she could count on her brother Charlie to help her, and she asked him to let her use one of the cottages on the Althorp estate for a country retreat. Charlie agreed at first, but changed his mind when he realized what heavy security the Princess of Wales would need. Diana was disappointed not to have the cottage, but much more upset that Charlie had turned her down. Charlie, the little brother she'd cuddled and looked after when their mother left! Diana felt a new sympathy for Raine, so harshly treated by Charlie.

Raine's mother, Barbara Cartland, was still steadily turning out her romance novels, and Diana was still reading them. In 1993 she had to smile over a new Barbara Cartland book, *The Queen of Hearts*. In this story, a beautiful, compassionate young woman marries the selfish, hard-hearted king of a small country. The people are on the verge of rebelling and dethroning the king, but his angelic bride wins their hearts. She also transforms her royal husband, through the power of love, into a model king. They all live happily ever after.

The situation reminded Diana of her first trip to Wales, when the prince and princess had been met with protests and threats of violence. Like Princess Sola in *The Queen of Hearts*, Diana was instinctively trusted by the people. The Welsh had fallen in love with her after only a few appearances and a procession.

The big difference was that Diana had not been able to make Charles fall madly in love with her, and she felt deeply rejected. For a long time Diana had wanted to leave Charles, but she was afraid of losing custody of William and Harry. As a child Diana hadn't been told that her mother, Frances, had lost custody of her children when she left Johnny Spencer for Peter Shand Kydd. Diana's father had been able to keep his children because the Spencer family was so powerful. How could Diana hope to win against the immense power of the British throne?

By the fall of 1993, William and Harry were

both at boarding school. When they were home at Kensington Palace with Diana, she cleared her social schedule to spend time with them. She encouraged them to invite friends for sleepovers. She often joined her sons for dinner or watched TV with them. Curled up on the green sofa in their sitting room, wearing a bathrobe but no makeup, Diana felt like a private person at last. The tabloids couldn't tell the world what she did here, and Buckingham Palace couldn't criticize her. She was free to be simply the young mother of two young boys.

Meanwhile, Diana still suffered from bulimia from time to time. She consulted an endless procession of experts: psychotherapists, tarot card readers, astrologers, aromatherapists, acupuncturists. Many of them seemed to help her for a while, but she never stayed with any treatment for long.

Although Diana was legally separated from Charles, she still had the title "Her Royal Highness, Princess of Wales." She was paid a salary, and she was still expected to follow a full schedule of official public appearances. In July 1993, Diana went on a tour in Zimbabwe, Africa. There, she comforted children with AIDS and helped publicize a leprosy mission. That same summer she took William and Harry to Walt Disney World, just for fun. Later that year she paid visits to royalty and political figures in Europe, and then attended a special service at Enniskillen in Northern Ireland, where a terrorist bomb had killed several people in 1987.

Diana assumed that by this time her privacy couldn't be invaded much further. She never suspected that a gym where she worked out might have hidden cameras. The first she knew was in November 1993, when the *Daily Mirror* published pictures of Diana in a leotard, working out. They had paid the manager of the gym over 100,000 pounds for the photographs.

Diana's reaction surprised many people. She announced that she was taking a break from public life. She was withdrawing from involvement in most of the charities she supported. In the coming year, she would make only a few appearances on the royal tour.

The queen and Prince Charles felt that Diana was making an unnecessary fuss. Because of her dramatic announcement, the tabloids spread rumors that Charles was trying to force Diana out of the spotlight. The queen decided not to include Diana in the annual festivities of Royal Ascot week, although that wasn't what Diana meant by "withdrawing."

About the same time as her announcement, Diana dropped the police security team that had protected her ever since her engagement to Prince Charles. Maybe she had the idea that if most of her official public appearances were canceled, the photographers and reporters would leave her alone. But it was just the opposite. Now that she was seen less in public, unofficial pictures of her were that much more valuable. The paparazzi followed her in ravenous packs. They even disguised themselves as waiters or clerks at restaurants and shops she was likely to go to.

It was difficult for Diana to know whom to trust. Anyone who got close to her could make a lot of money by selling whatever they knew about her. One of the worst offenders was James Hewitt, who sold the story of his romance with her to a journalist. The resulting book, *Princess in Love*, was published in October 1994.

In royal circles, there were many courtiers who were Diana's enemies. Friends of Charles urged him to defend himself against *Diana: Her True Story* by letting his own story be published. Finally in June 1994, *The Prince of Wales*, an authorized biography of Charles written by Jonathan Dimbleby, came out. An accompanying TV documentary, *Charles: The Private Man, The Public Role*, was released at the same time. The biography and documentary were advertised as a celebration of Charles's twenty-fifth anniversary as Prince of Wales, but obviously they were also a reply to *Diana: Her True Story*.

More than anything else, the documentary

showed that Charles did not understand how to use the media. Charles thought the public would be more sympathetic to him if he was honest, so he admitted on camera that he'd had an affair with a former girlfriend. This discussion took only seconds out of the two-and-a-half-hour documentary, but it was the only thing the public paid any attention to.

The same night that Charles's documentary ran on TV, Diana appeared at a *Vanity Fair* party in one of her smashing outfits, a low-cut black evening dress sprinkled with jewels. She wore one of her favorite necklaces, an enormous sapphire set in diamonds and mounted on a pearl choker. It was as if she were saying to her fans, "Why would Prince Charles want any other woman when he's married to *me*?" The public agreed with her. Charles's attempt to explain his side of the marriage only made him look worse.

Even though Charles was much less critical of her in the authorized biography than she had been of him, Diana felt Dimbleby had portrayed her as mentally unstable. She was very angry.

She stewed about it for a year, then appeared on TV on *Panorama*, a British public affairs program, on November 20, 1995. Her friends and advisers had urged her not to give this interview, because they thought it would only damage her relationship with the royal family even further. But Fergie encouraged Diana to go ahead, and so did Rita Rogers, a psychic Diana consulted. Diana liked that advice better.

On *Panorama*, Diana appeared calm and intelligent. She wore a simple dark suit and white shirt, and her pale makeup and dark eyeliner emphasized her seriousness. Most of the interview was about how miserable Diana's marriage to Charles had been. Speaking in a well-controlled voice, she gave graphic descriptions of her eating disorder, bulimia. She stated that both she and Charles had been unfaithful in their marriage. She even suggested that it might be best for Charles to give up his claim to the throne and let William become the next King of England.

As for her own future, what did Diana

intend to do with her life now? She still wanted a public role, as an "unofficial ambassador" for Britain. She would "go out there and love people and show it." Diana knew she would never become Queen of England, as she had once expected. But she still hoped to be the "queen of people's hearts."

Diana's sensible friends were right about the royal family's reaction. It was bad enough for her to leak information to Andrew Morton for *Diana: Her True Story*. It was much worse for her to announce the same embarrassing information on national television. Furthermore, Diana had not asked the queen's permission, as was customary, to give the interview. She hadn't even notified Buckingham Palace until the week before the program ran.

But Diana was once again using the media to get the public on her side. And the public, especially women, loved Diana more than ever. The day after the *Panorama* program, the *Sun*'s headline ran, YOU WERE MAGNIFICENT DI: THOUSANDS CALL THE *SUN* TO PRAISE BRAVE PRINCESS.

The queen and her advisers at Buckingham Palace saw Diana's *Panorama* interview as an attack on them as well as on Charles. The whole royal family drew together in defense. Even Princess Margaret, who had been Diana's best supporter inside the royal family, wrote her an angry letter. In December the queen wrote both Diana and Charles, and she did not mince words: The two of them were to work out an "early divorce . . . in the best interests of the country."

They began that painful process with a private meeting in February 1996, and the divorce became final that August. Diana and Charles would keep joint custody of their children. Diana would continue to live at Kensington Palace and have offices at St. James's Palace. Diana would receive a financial settlement of 28 million pounds, plus a yearly salary for her official duties. Diana's title from that point on would be "Diana, Princess of Wales," not "Her Royal Highness."

Diana had ended 1995 with a trip to New

York City, where she received the United Cerebral Palsy (UCP) Humanitarian of the Year Award. The event was also a fund-raiser, netting more than $2 million for the UCP organization. Early in 1996, while the terms of the divorce were being worked out, Diana flew to Pakistan to visit a cancer hospital. She then flew to Chicago to help raise money for the fight against breast cancer. At Diana's every appearance in Chicago, big crowds cheered her, and her spirits rose.

But Diana was confused. Her publicity was out of control. She didn't know whom to trust, and she wouldn't listen to anyone who disagreed with her. On July 1, 1996, she turned thirty-five. On July 15, Diana and Charles filed their divorce papers. Shortly afterward, Diana announced that she was cutting back on the number of charities she worked with. When Diana was criticized for this, she blamed her new media adviser, who left.

CHAPTER 15

THE QUEEN OF HEARTS

Diana's marriage to Charles, the main focus of her adult life, was over for good. She needed a new focus, and she searched for a cause to make use of her worldwide celebrity. She decided to join the movement, led by the Red Cross, to ban land mines.

In the aftermath of wars—the civil wars in Cambodia, Bosnia, Afghanistan, and Angola, for instance—the land had been left booby-trapped by explosives. Innocent people, often children, were regularly killed and maimed by mines. In Angola alone there were more buried mines waiting to blow up innocent victims than there were people in the country.

In January 1997, Diana flew to Angola, in southwest Africa. A BBC television crew flew with her to film the visit. Diana, the fashion queen, wore a simple white shirt and chino pants. From Luanda, the capital city, she traveled to places still riddled with minefields. Diana visited a hospital and stopped by the beds of land mine victims. One girl, Helena, was almost dead, her insides blown out.

It was wrenching for Diana to see such dreadful suffering. But that was why she was there. Because Diana, a wildly popular celebrity, was filmed by Helena's bedside, millions of TV viewers would also see Helena's suffering. Perhaps then public opinion against land mines would force governments to ban their use.

And besides, Diana could offer her extraordinary gift for comforting. After Diana had left the hospital, Helena asked a journalist, "Who was that? Is she an angel?" The girl died soon afterward.

Later Diana was filmed walking through a minefield herself. She wore a face visor and flak jacket, but they would not have protected her very well if a mine had exploded underneath her feet. After she finished, some photographers asked her to do the walk again so they could get better shots. Diana cheerfully agreed. That was why she was there: to create pictures that would convince the nations of the world to give up land mines.

After her trip to Angola, Diana planned similar trips for the Red Cross to Afghanistan, Bosnia, and Cambodia. In the meantime, she had a different kind of charity work going. She donated seventy-nine of her designer dresses to an auction in New York City, to raise money for the AIDS Crisis Trust. Diana was proud that it had been William's idea to sell the dresses for charity. The auction in June was a great success, raising more than $3 million.

As for Diana and Charles, they got along much better now that they were divorced. That spring they even traveled together to William's confirmation ceremony. Sitting side by side, they were able to behave in a friendly way to each other.

Sadly, Diana quarreled with many of the

other people she used to be close to. She was a good friend of the pop singer Elton John, and at first she agreed to help publicize his new book *Rock and Royalty*, a fund-raiser for his AIDS Foundation. But then she saw the photos in the book, which included some of naked men as well as of the royal family. The queen would certainly consider it undignified for anyone in the royal family—even an estranged ex-daughter-in-law—to be associated with this book.

Although Diana had already outraged the queen with the Andrew Morton biography and her appearance on *Panorama*, she hesitated to offend her further. Diana withdrew her support from *Rock and Royalty*. When Elton John reacted angrily, she stopped speaking to him.

Diana's friendship with Sarah Ferguson also ended shortly after her divorce from Charles. Diana had been especially close to Fergie in the years before her divorce, sharing inside jokes and rants about the royal family as no one else could. But then in November 1996,

Fergie had published her autobiography, *My Story*. Diana was outraged at some of her "friend's" comments about her. Fergie even mentioned that she'd gotten warts from borrowing Diana's boots. Diana was so hurt and angry that, from then on, she wouldn't allow Sarah Ferguson's name to be mentioned in her presence.

In May 1997, Diana was horrified to read an interview with her mother in the British magazine *Hello!* Part of the interview was about Diana, and not all of it was favorable. To Diana's anger, Frances criticized Diana for talking about her marriage problems in the *Panorama* interview. Frances also criticized Charles for doing the same in his TV interview—but then she further hurt Diana by saying she was still on friendly terms with her son-in-law Prince Charles. Diana never spoke to her mother again.

Diana was lonely. She called her sons at school every day and spent her vacations with them, but they were growing up. William was now fifteen, and Harry almost thirteen. Diana talked to friends about possibly finding true love and having another child.

In July 1997, Diana accepted an invitation from Mohamed al Fayed, the owner of Harrods department store, to come with her sons for a holiday on his yacht in the Mediterranean. She thought that the wealthy merchant would be able to give them privacy as well as a luxurious vacation. On the *Jonikal*, Fayed's yacht, she met his oldest son, Dodi.

Dodi was a charming and handsome playboy, with plenty of money and time to spend on romance. He was engaged to an American fashion model, but he broke that off for Diana. Later in July the two met again in Paris, where they were photographed kissing in public, and Diana took another cruise with Dodi on his father's yacht.

At the beginning of August, Diana flew to Bosnia to publicize the land mine problem in that country. Toward the end of the month, as William and Harry went to Balmoral with the royal family, she went off for another vacation with Dodi al Fayed. They cruised on the *Jonikal* again, and then flew to Paris. The tabloids ran pictures of the couple on the yacht and in Paris. DI'S SECRET HOL WITH HARROD'S HUNK DODI was the *Sun*'s headline on August 7. Dodi's ex-fiancée sold *her* story to the tabloids for more than $300,000.

Apparently Dodi thought that Diana was going to accept an engagement ring from him. Diana, however, told several friends that she and Dodi were just having a good time. "Don't worry," she reassured them. "I need another marriage like a bad rash on my face."

The media were frantic to get fresh news about Diana and the playboy, Harrods heir. On the evening of August 30, a mob of photographers jostled outside Dodi's Paris apartment. When Dodi and Diana left for a restaurant, they followed in a pack.

Obviously Dodi and Diana wouldn't be able to dine in privacy at the restaurant, so they went on to the Ritz hotel. Again they were followed by the paparazzi. By this time

Dodi was in a rage, and Diana was crying.

After eating dinner in a private suite, the couple left again shortly after midnight, and they headed back to Dodi's apartment. Dodi's real chauffeur drove a decoy car with his two bodyguards, to get the photographers to follow them. Meanwhile, Dodi, Diana, and a bodyguard sneaked out the back entrance of the Ritz in a rented Mercedes, driven by the deputy security chief of the hotel.

But the paparazzi were not so easy to fool, and some of them waited for the couple outside the back entrance. They chased Dodi and Diana's car at high speed through the streets of Paris. At a dangerous spot in the tunnel under the Place d'Alma, the driver apparently lost control. The Mercedes crashed into one of the concrete pillars.

Dodi and the driver were killed instantly in the crash. Afterward, the Paris police determined that none of the passengers had worn seat belts, and that the driver had been drunk. The bodyguard was severely hurt, but eventually survived. Diana was taken to a hospital and given emergency care, but she was so badly injured that the medical team could not save her. By four o'clock on the morning of August 31, the most photographed woman in the world was dead.

As the sad news spread, mourners in every part of the globe sat stunned in front of their TV sets. In London, crowds gathered in front of Buckingham Palace. They brought flowers, thousands of bouquets, with loving notes and prayers for their princess. They camped out at the palace gates, finding comfort with strangers by crying and hugging one another.

The grieving crowds began to notice that the royal family, still at Balmoral, didn't seem to be mourning with them. Prince Charles was photographed riding in a limousine with his sons—without putting his arms around them. The queen had made no statement about Diana's death, and the flag in front of Buckingham Palace had not been lowered.

People began to get angry, and Charles's

advisers predicted there might be ugly demon-strations. The queen and Charles might be booed at Diana's funeral. There could be riots in London.

Diana would have known just how to act in such a situation. Without stopping to think it over, she would have shown the people that she shared their sorrow. But the royal family was stunned and baffled. Fortunately, Prime Minister Tony Blair understood, and he encouraged the queen to do what the populace thought was fitting for the death of a national heroine.

On Friday, the flag outside Buckingham Palace was lowered to half-mast. Charles, William, and Harry came to London to mingle with people on the streets and thank them for their sympathy. The day before the funeral, Queen Elizabeth appeared on television to give tribute to her former daughter-in-law. From the queen's point of view, Diana had been a problem for the royal family ever since her wedding. But now she praised Diana as "an exceptional and gifted human being." Elizabeth went on to say, "I admired and respected her for her energy and commitment to others."

Meanwhile, Diana's body lay in state in St. James's Chapel Royal, where she had attended her Grandmother Cynthia's memorial service long ago. The funeral was held in Westminster Abbey on Sunday, September 7. Like Diana's wedding, Diana's funeral was televised and broadcast around the world, and more than 2 billion people watched it. Elton John, his quarrel with the princess forgotten, sang his song for Diana, "Goodbye, England's Rose." Charlie Spencer, the coolness between him and Diana also forgotten, gave a passionate elegy for the sister who had protected and comforted him years ago.

After the service, Diana's body was taken to Althorp for burial. Grieving crowds stood along the whole eighty-mile route, showering the hearse with flowers. Diana was buried on the island in the lake where she used to retreat at Althorp.

In November 1997, the Nobel Peace Prize was awarded to the International Campaign against Land Mines. One hundred and twenty-two countries signed a ban on land mines.

Princess Diana, through her very public openness about her own feelings and her compassion for others, had changed the culture of her nation. The British, famous for keeping a stiff upper lip no matter how much they were suffering, would never be the same. Neither would the British monarchy, pulled down from its pedestal by "the people's princess." The queen announced that bowing and curtsying to the royal family was no longer compulsory. That meant, for one thing, that Prince William's and Harry's future girlfriends would not have to call them "sir."

Also, the old class system in British society was breaking down. The government decided that hereditary peers (which included Diana's brother, the ninth Earl Spencer) would not automatically become members of the House of Lords in Parliament.

FOR MORE INFORMATION

VIDEO

A&E Biography.
  Diana: The True Story.
  A&E Home Video, 1998.
  Includes many pictures from Diana's
  childhood; interviews with several people
  close to Diana during different periods
  of her life; and film clips of Diana herself.

BOOKS

Graham, Tim.
  Diana: H.R.H. The Princess of Wales.
  New York: Summit Books, 1988.
  Diana in photographs, from the "Shy Di" of
  1980 to the glamorous fashion icon of 1988.

Landau, Elaine.
Land Mines: 100 Million Hidden Killers.
Berkeley Heights, NJ: Enslow Publishers, 2000.
Describes dangers of, the fight to stop production of, and efforts to remove land mines and help their victims.

ON THE INTERNET

http://www.althorp.com
The official Web site of the Spencers' ancestral estate, which was Diana's home from ages fourteen through seventeen, and is now the site of her grave.

http://www.royal.gov.uk
A thorough source of information about English royalty, including the present royal family and key figures in the history of the English monarchy.

http://www.unicef.org/graca/mines.htm
A concise explanation of the horrific
worldwide problem of land mines.

FOR ADULT READERS

Burrell, Paul.
A Royal Duty.
New York: G. P. Putnam's Sons, 2003.
By Diana's butler, previously Queen
Elizabeth's footman. Many behind-the-scenes
details about the everyday lives of Diana,
Charles, and the Queen.

Clayton, Tim, and Phil Craig.
Diana: Story of a Princess.
New York: Pocket Books, 2001.
An evenhanded biography of Princess
Diana, emphasizing her tormented
private life, her spectacular success with
the public, and her love-hate relationship
with the media.

Edwards, Anne.
 Ever After: Diana and the Life She Led.
 New York: St. Martin's Press, 2000.
 As *Booklist* described this biography, "A
 competent, compact life story that gives all
 the details without wallowing in them."